Y0-BCM-056

High-Energy Meetings for Young Teenagers

Loveland, Colorado

High-Energy Meetings for Young Teenagers

Copyright © 1999 Group Publishing, Inc.

All rights reserved. No part of this book may be reproduced in any manner whatsoever without prior written permission from the publisher, except where noted in the text and in the case of brief quotations embodied in critical articles and reviews. For information, write Permissions, Group Publishing, Inc., Dept. PD, P.O. Box 481, Loveland, CO 80539.

Visit our Web site: **www.grouppublishing.com**

Credits
Many thanks to all the authors who contributed to Jr. High Ministry Magazine over the years.
Book Acquisitions Editor: Amy Simpson
Editor: Debbie Gowensmith
Quality Control Editor: Dave Thornton
Chief Creative Officer: Joani Schultz
Copy Editor: Patti Leach
Art Director: Desktop Miracles
Cover Art Director: Jeff A. Storm
Computer Graphic Artist: Anita Cook
Cover Designer: Alan Furst
Illustrator: Pat David
Production Manager: Alexander Jorgensen

Unless otherwise noted, Scripture taken from the HOLY BIBLE, NEW INTERNATIONAL VERSION®. Copyright © 1973, 1978, 1984 by International Bible Society. Used by permission of Zondervan Publishing House. All rights reserved.

Library of Congress Cataloging-in-Publication Data
High-energy meetings for young teenagers.
      p.   cm.
   Includes indexes.
   ISBN 0-7644-2083-6 (alk. paper)
   1. Church group work with teenagers. 2. Junior high school
students--Religious life. I. Group Publishing.
BV4447.H49 1999
259' .23--dc21   99-21807
                                               CIP

10 9 8 7 6 5 4 3 2 1   08 07 06 05 04 03 02 01 00 99

Printed in the United States of America.

Contents

Introduction

Junior highers are going through changes and life events unique to their age group. They need special attention to what they're dealing with, in a way they can understand. Use the meetings in *High-Energy Meetings for Young Teenagers* to address your junior highers' special needs.

These meetings come to you from people all around the United States who work with junior highers and understand their unique developmental stage. The authors also understand what it's like for you to work with this age group. They know what it's like to plan a junior high meeting the same week taxes are due, baseball tryouts begin, and a piano recital occurs. They provide clear, ample instructions and almost always use easy-to-obtain supplies for low-preparation meetings.

Just because meetings are short on preparation time doesn't mean they're short on substance. In forty-five to sixty minutes, your junior highers will actively discover biblical truths that affect their lives. They'll dig into Scripture, *experience* the meaning of Scripture, and apply what they experience to their lives. With the tools they gather from these meetings, your young teenagers will be equipped with a fresh outlook on how their faith directs their lives.

To help you quickly choose meetings relevant to your group, we've included two indexes. A Scripture index will help you find meetings that encourage your teenagers to understand and apply a particular passage of Scripture. A theme index will help you find meetings about issues your group needs or wants to delve into.

We've also divided the book into these three sections:

- The "Building Faith" section, with meetings about topics such as Christian growth and making Jesus the center of life, helps your junior highers grow a deep, lasting faith based on an understanding of what the Christian faith is about.

- The "Growing Up" section, with meetings about topics such as body image and drug use, addresses choices and attitudes especially relevant to junior highers. These meetings will affect how your teenagers act out their faith in daily choices.

- The "Celebrating Holidays" section, with meetings about topics such as justice for Easter and giving for Christmas, encourages your junior highers to experience the true meaning of holidays. Instead of merely celebrating, your young teenagers can deepen their faith during holiday seasons.

High-Energy Meetings for Young Teenagers, the best ideas from the magazine devoted to junior highers' faith, will help your young teenagers transition into independence with a strong faith and a strong commitment to Christian values.

Section 1

BUILDING FAITH

Bringing the Bible to Life: Part 1

THEMES

Bible, Self-Image, Spiritual Growth

SCRIPTURE

Psalm 139;
Matthew 10:29-31;
Galatians 5:19-21;
James 1:22-25

LEADER TIP

If you have an Avon or a Mary Kay cosmetics salesperson in your church, perhaps you can get lipstick samples to use for this activity.

Why This Meeting Is Important

A rule book. A history book. A textbook. That's how many junior highers view the Bible, and they're not very excited about it. Many of the Bible's own descriptions of itself may not seem personally relevant to junior highers: a lamp to our feet, honey, a two-edged sword. But a mirror—that's something junior highers depend on daily! Use this lesson to show junior highers how the Bible speaks directly *to* them and *about* them.

What Students Will Learn

In this meeting junior highers will
- discover how the Bible can act as a mirror,
- see how they can get an "accurate reflection" of who they are from the Bible, and
- reflect on how they can use the Bible as a mirror in the coming week.

Before the Meeting

Read the meeting, and gather supplies.

Supplies

You'll need Bibles, aluminum foil, scissors, pens, pencils, and paper. Additional supplies for optional activities: a hand mirror, tubes of lipstick, straight razors without blades or with safety caps on, a can of shaving cream, and paper towels.

Choose Your Opener

Opener Option 1: Mirror, Mirror

You'll need a Bible, a hand mirror, a tube of lipstick for each guy, a straight razor—without the blade or with a safety cap on—for each girl, a can of shaving cream, and paper towels.

As teenagers arrive, have them look at themselves in the hand mirror for ten seconds. After everyone has looked in the mirror, have the guys line up facing the girls, and give each guy a tube of lipstick. Say: **Now that you've looked in the mirror, let's see how well you remember your face. Put on this lipstick.** Have the girls judge who does the best job. Then give each girl a dollop of shaving cream and a straight razor (without the blade or with the safety cap on), and let the girls "shave" the cream off their faces. Have the guys judge who does the best job.

Read aloud James 1:22-25. Ask:

- **How is this passage like the experience you just had?**
- **In what ways is the Bible like a mirror?**

Have teenagers clean off their faces with the paper towels.

Opener Option 2: Mirror Images

You'll need a Bible.

Have teenagers choose partners. Say: **We're going to do a classic drama exercise called mirroring. Face your partner. Choose one person in your pair to be the actor. The other partner must mirror any actions the actor makes. For example, if the actor raises her right hand, the "mirror" will raise her left hand just as if the actor were seeing her reflection in a mirror. Don't look around at the other pairs; just look at each other. Go.**

After a few minutes, have the partners switch roles.

After both partners have had a turn as actor and as mirror, ask:

- **What was it like to see your partner doing everything you did?**
- **Did anything about this activity make you self-conscious? Explain.**
- **If someone reflected back to you all your actions in real life, what would you learn about yourself?**

Read aloud James 1:22-25. Ask:

- **How is this passage like the experience you just had?**
- **In what ways is the Bible like a mirror?**

Bible Experience: Beauties and Blemishes

You'll need Bibles, squares of aluminum foil, and pens.

Give each person a Bible, a square of aluminum foil, and a pen. Say: **Mirrors can show us positive things about ourselves, such as smiles or a new outfit we look great in. Mirrors can also show us things we need to take care of, such as unzipped zippers or messed-up hair. The Bible does the same thing. It reflects the beautiful love God has for us by telling how God sent his Son to save us from our sin. It also teaches us how we should respond to that love and warns us about blemishes we need to take care of.**

LEADER TIP

Even if it seems to interrupt the flow of your meeting, be sure to let teenagers clean up. Until they get their faces back to normal, they'll be too self-conscious to concentrate on anything else.

Imagine that your piece of foil is a mirror. On the shinier side, write three words that reflect what the Bible says about you in Psalm 139 and Matthew 10:29-31. On the duller side, write three words that reflect the blemishes the Bible warns you to look out for in Galatians 5:19-21. Then, on each side of the foil, draw a picture or symbol that portrays the words you wrote on that side. Be as creative as you like with both pictures, using symbols, word labels, and anything else you can think of to communicate the meaning of those words.

When everyone has finished, have teenagers find partners and explain their drawings to each other.

Reflection: Good Grooming

You'll need pencils and paper.

Have teenagers stay with their partners. Give each pair a sheet of paper and a pencil. Say: **With your partner, list ways a mirror reflects what you look like on the outside. For example, you might use a mirror when you brush your teeth to make sure you don't leave any food stuck between your teeth. Then list ways the Bible reflects who you are on the inside. For example, the Bible says we're sinners in need of God's forgiveness.**

Give partners about three minutes, and then have them share their lists with the rest of the group. Then challenge teenagers this week to look up at least two of the words from their Bible-related lists in a concordance, find the verses in the Bible, and read them. You might want to review how to use a concordance. Have teenagers practice by finding one word from their lists.

Suggest that students put their aluminum foil "mirrors" on their real mirrors at home as reminders to turn to the Bible to get a true reflection of themselves from God's Word.

Choose Your Closing

Closing Option 1: A Nice Reflection on You

Have students stay with their partners. Say: **We've seen that ordinary mirrors reflect what we look like on the outside and that the Bible reflects what we're like on the inside. Tell your partner one positive thing he or she would see in a mirror that reflects his or her personality or character. For example, you might say, "Your reflection would show your great sense of humor."**

Closing Option 2: Reflected Love

You'll need a hand mirror.

Have students form a circle, and read aloud Matthew 10:29-31. Say: **The**

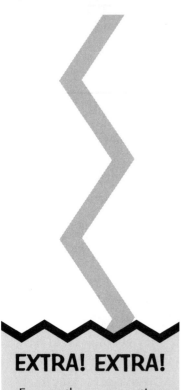

EXTRA! EXTRA!

For another perspective on the Bible as a mirror, have teenagers read 1 Corinthians 13:8-12, where God says the love we see reflected in the Bible will be even more dazzling when we see God face to face.

Bible is a mirror that shows us we're people God loves. When someone passes you the mirror, hold it up to the person on your right so that person can see his or her reflection. Then say, "[Name], the person you see is a person God loves" before passing the mirror to the next person. Pass the mirror around the circle.

Bringing the Bible to Life: Part 2

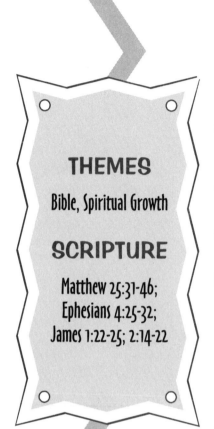

THEMES

Bible, Spiritual Growth

SCRIPTURE

Matthew 25:31-46;
Ephesians 4:25-32;
James 1:22-25; 2:14-22

Why This Meeting Is Important

"Why should I learn this?" "What does this have to do with my life?" "When am I ever going to use this?"

Junior highers ask these questions about math, history—and the Bible. Use this lesson to help teenagers apply the Bible to their lives in practical ways.

What Students Will Learn

In this meeting junior highers will

- discover different ways to respond to the Bible and
- compile a devotional booklet to help them read and apply the Bible in the coming week.

Before the Meeting

Read the meeting, and gather supplies. Write each of the following statements on a separate sheet of paper, and tape the papers around the room:

- "A promise I can claim"
- "A command I should obey"
- "A good example for me to follow"
- "A bad example for me to avoid"
- "A sin in my life I need to confess"
- "A feeling or situation I identify with"
- "A new thought about God"

Supplies

You'll need Bibles, paper, a marker, tape, pencils, a stapler, scissors, photocopies of the "Devotional Page Instructions" handout (p. 16), and access to a photocopy machine.

Additional supplies for optional activities: old magazines and markers.

Choose Your Opener

Opener Option 1: Manic Makeovers

You'll need a Bible, old magazines, and markers.

Have students form groups of three. Hand out magazines and markers. Say: **In your trio, find a picture of an attractive model to tear out of the magazine. Then take two minutes to give the model a makeover by drawing on the picture, but make the model look worse. Everyone should contribute to the makeover.**

After two minutes, have the trios display their made-over models. Ask:

- **If these models saw themselves in a mirror, what do you think they'd do?**
- **What would you think of a model who went straight to a photo shoot without doing anything about how he or she looked?**

Read aloud James 1:22-25. Then ask:

- **How is the person in this passage like the model we talked about?**
- **In what ways do you forget what you learn in the Bible?**

Say: **Today we're going to explore some ways to look into the Bible and act on what we see.**

Opener Option 2: Mr. and Ms. Short-Term Memory

You'll need a Bible.

Have students form groups of four. Say: *Saturday Night Live* used to have a character called Mr. Short-Term Memory. He couldn't remember anything for longer than two seconds. He'd hold a match until it burned him because he didn't remember he'd lit it, and he'd spit out food because he didn't remember he'd put it in his mouth. You're going to improvise—or act without planning what you're going to do—as if we're like that. Pretend you're Mr. or Ms. Short-Term Memory. When it's your group's turn, I'll give you a situation and have you act for a minute.

One at a time, give each group a situation to improvise for one minute. After each group has performed, ask:

- **What was it like to act as if you couldn't remember anything?**
- **What kinds of problems do people in real life have if they don't remember important things?**

Read aloud James 1:22-25, and then ask:

- **How is the person in this passage like Mr. or Ms. Short-Term Memory?**
- **In what ways do you tend to forget what you learn from the Bible?**

Say: **Today we're going to explore some ways to follow instead of forget what God tells us in the Bible.**

LEADER TIP

Give groups situations with potential for humor—for example, skiing (teenagers can forget they're on the towrope and let go) or dining out (teenagers can ask the server to repeat the kinds of salad dressing again and again).

LEADER TIP

Students with the same passage may stand by different signs. Assure students that passages have several applications, so there isn't one right answer.

Bible Experience: Follow the Signs

You'll need Bibles and the signs you posted before the meeting.

Give everyone a Bible. Assign each person one of the following passages: Matthew 25:31-46; Ephesians 4:25-32; James 2:14-22. Say: **Read your passage silently and find something in the passage that matches one of the signs posted around the room. Some passages will have only one match, and some may match all the signs. Here's an example.** Read aloud James 1:22-25. Say: **This passage has a command: Don't just listen to God's Word, but do it (verse 22). It also has a promise: If I obey God's commands, I will be blessed (verse 25). Now read your passage, and stand under a sign that describes something you found in the passage.**

When everyone has moved to a sign, ask volunteers to read aloud their passages and tell why they chose the sign they did. Then have everyone reread their passages and move to another sign if they see another application.

Reflection: Devotional Writing

You'll need Bibles, pencils, paper, a stapler, scissors, and photocopies of the "Devotional Page Instructions" handout (p. 16). You'll also need access to a photocopy machine.

Have students get into pairs. Say: **We're going to make a devotional book. Each pair will write one page of the book. We'll photocopy all the pages, staple them together, and use the book to help us read and apply the Bible this week.**

Give each pair a sheet of paper and a pencil. Say: **With your partner, choose a short Bible passage—no more than two or three verses. You may choose a section of one of the passages we just read or a favorite passage of your own. Then follow these instructions to write your devotional page.** Distribute the "Devotional Page Instructions" handouts.

As pairs finish their devotional pages, make enough copies for everyone to have one. Have teenagers staple complete sets together to take home. Encourage teenagers to read and act on the challenges their friends have written.

Choose Your Closing

Closing Option 1: Partner Prayer

Have students stay with their partners. Say: **Tell your partner one specific way you hope to meet a challenge in our devotional booklet. For example, if the challenge was to compliment someone you sometimes envy, tell your partner who you'll compliment and what you'll say. Then pray for each other, asking God to help you meet the challenge.**

Closing Option 2: Circle Prayer

Have students form a circle and stand next to their partners from the devotion-writing activity. Pray by having partners read aloud the prayers they wrote. Close the prayer by asking God to motivate teenagers to read the devotional book faithfully this week and to carry out the challenges.

DEVOTIONAL PAGE INSTRUCTIONS

- Write the reference for your passage—for example, "Ephesians 4:29."
- Write a short sentence or phrase that describes what this passage makes you feel or think about—for example, "I guess it's not enough to avoid saying mean things; God wants me to say things that will make people feel good."
- Write at least two challenges to apply this passage in specific ways this week—for example, "Thank Mom or Dad for something they do for me" and "Compliment someone I sometimes envy."
- Write a prayer, either thanking God for a promise he made in your passage or asking him to help you with the challenges you wrote.

DEVOTIONAL PAGE INSTRUCTIONS

- Write the reference for your passage—for example, "Ephesians 4:29."
- Write a short sentence or phrase that describes what this passage makes you feel or think about—for example, "I guess it's not enough to avoid saying mean things; God wants me to say things that will make people feel good."
- Write at least two challenges to apply this passage in specific ways this week—for example, "Thank Mom or Dad for something they do for me" and "Compliment someone I sometimes envy."
- Write a prayer, either thanking God for a promise he made in your passage or asking him to help you with the challenges you wrote.

DEVOTIONAL PAGE INSTRUCTIONS

- Write the reference for your passage—for example, "Ephesians 4:29."
- Write a short sentence or phrase that describes what this passage makes you feel or think about—for example, "I guess it's not enough to avoid saying mean things; God wants me to say things that will make people feel good."
- Write at least two challenges to apply this passage in specific ways this week—for example, "Thank Mom or Dad for something they do for me" and "Compliment someone I sometimes envy."
- Write a prayer, either thanking God for a promise he made in your passage or asking him to help you with the challenges you wrote.

DEVOTIONAL PAGE INSTRUCTIONS

- Write the reference for your passage—for example, "Ephesians 4:29."
- Write a short sentence or phrase that describes what this passage makes you feel or think about—for example, "I guess it's not enough to avoid saying mean things; God wants me to say things that will make people feel good."
- Write at least two challenges to apply this passage in specific ways this week—for example, "Thank Mom or Dad for something they do for me" and "Compliment someone I sometimes envy."
- Write a prayer, either thanking God for a promise he made in your passage or asking him to help you with the challenges you wrote.

Permission to photocopy this handout from *High-Energy Meetings for Young Teenagers* granted for local church use.
Copyright © Group Publishing, Inc., P.O. Box 481, Loveland, CO 80539.

Building a Friendship With Jesus

Why This Meeting Is Important

Almost all junior highers say that having reliable friends is very important. Unfortunately, most junior highers don't realize they can be best friends with the most reliable friend alive. Use this meeting to help teenagers build a friendship with that person: Jesus.

What Students Will Learn

In this meeting junior highers will
- identify the qualities of a perfect friend,
- discuss things to do with Jesus, and
- commit to becoming better friends with Jesus.

Before the Meeting

Read the meeting, and gather supplies. On separate index cards, write ten qualities of a friend, such as "loyalty" or "good listening skills," and ten things friends do together, such as "goof off" or "talk on the phone." Place each card in an envelope, and hide the envelopes around the room. If you choose the "Good Match" closing, make a peanut butter and jelly sandwich, a peanut butter and toothpaste sandwich, and a peanut butter and wrench sandwich.

Supplies

You'll need Bibles, index cards, a marker, envelopes, pencils, paper, and photocopies of the "Ad in the Personals" handout (p. 20).

Additional supplies for optional activities: bread, peanut butter, jelly, toothpaste, a wrench, a table knife, a plate, and a small prize.

THEMES

Friendship, Jesus

SCRIPTURE

John 11:1-43; 15:13-15

Choose Your Opener

Opener Option 1: Make-a-Friend Contest

You'll need a small prize.

Give teenagers sixty seconds to ask as many people as possible what their birthdays and favorite foods are—without writing down the answers. Then have students form a circle and take turns trying to remember what they heard. Award a small prize to the person who remembers the most birthdays and foods.

Say: **If making friends were as easy as asking a person's birthday and favorite food, we'd have plenty of friends. But making new friends involves more than just asking questions, even when that friend is Jesus. Today we're going to learn more about building a friendship with Jesus.**

Opener Option 2: Paper Airplane Partnerships

You'll need paper.

Have students form pairs. Have partners stand shoulder to shoulder and lock their inside arms. Give each pair a sheet of paper, and have pairs make paper airplanes using only their free hands. After students have finished, have a contest to see which airplane flies the farthest.

Say: **Some tasks seem impossible, such as making a paper airplane with one hand. But a friend can make the impossible happen, especially if that friend is Jesus. Today we're going to learn more about building a friendship with Jesus.**

Bible Experience: Pursuing a Perfect Friend

You'll need Bibles, the envelopes you prepared and hid around the room before the meeting, pencils, and paper.

Have students form groups of no more than six. Say: **People are always looking for the perfect friend. In this room, I've hidden sealed envelopes that contain information about a perfect friend. You have three minutes to find the envelopes, but don't open them.**

After three minutes, ask teenagers with envelopes to open them, one at a time, and read aloud the enclosed cards. Then ask students to tell other qualities of a perfect friend and other things to do with a friend. Ask:

- How was hunting for envelopes like or unlike hunting for friends? Explain.
- Which of these qualities of a friend does Jesus bring into a friendship?
- How do Jesus' qualities compare with your other friends' qualities?
- How can you do with Jesus the things you do with other friends?

Give each group a Bible, a pencil, and paper. On their papers, have groups make two columns: "Jesus" and "Jesus' Friends." Have groups read aloud John 11:1-43. As they read, have them list under the appropriate headings the friendship qualities of Jesus and his friends. Afterward ask:

- **How does Jesus show his friendship to us?**
- **How can we show our friendship to Jesus?**

Reflection: An Ad in the Personals

You'll need a Bible, photocopies of the "Ad in the Personals" handout (p. 20), and pencils.

Give each person an "Ad in the Personals" handout and a pencil. Ask students each to complete the ad. Afterward, have students read aloud their ads. Then read aloud John 15:13-15. Ask:

- **Why does Jesus want to be your friend?**
- **What are the advantages of having a friend like Jesus? What are the disadvantages?**
- **What are your responsibilities in a friendship with Jesus?**

Choose Your Closing

Closing Option 1: A Good Match

You'll need the sandwiches you prepared before the meeting.

Set out the sandwiches, and describe each sandwich. Have students vote for which sandwich they'd most like to eat. Ask:

- **Are toothpaste and wrenches good substitutes for jelly? Why or why not?**

Say: **Some people will tell you that popularity, money, and friends are good substitutes for Jesus. But just as peanut butter and jelly are the best match for a sandwich, Jesus and you are the best match for a friendship. If you agree, tell that to Jesus as we close in prayer.** Give teenagers a minute to pray silently.

Closing Option 2: Getting to Know Him

You'll need paper and pencils.

Have teenagers form groups of three. Give each group a sheet of paper and a pencil. Ask groups to list five things they can do to get to know Jesus better. Have teenagers each choose one thing they'll do and then share with the group how they'll do it. Then close in prayer, asking God to help teenagers follow through.

EXTRA! EXTRA!

- Have teenagers create a skit titled "How to Lose Friends and Alienate People." After the skit, lead a discussion of the things that can damage a friendship with Jesus.

- Have volunteers stand and finish the sentence, "One thing I like about having Jesus as a friend is..."

LEADER TIP

Some students will vote for the gross sandwiches to get attention, but the majority will pick peanut butter and jelly. If students do pick the gross sandwiches, have teenagers discuss how and why they sometimes have trouble making the best friendship choices.

An Ad in the Personals

Help Jesus write an ad to find a new friend.

WANTED: NEW FRIENDS FOR THE CREATOR OF THE UNIVERSE

Should be . . . _____

_____

_____

_____

_____

Should like . . . _____

_____

_____

_____

_____

Should want to . . . _____

_____

_____

_____

_____

PLEASE CALL 1-800-PRAYERS.

Permission to photocopy this handout from *High-Energy Meetings for Young Teenagers* granted for local church use.
Copyright © Group Publishing, Inc., P.O. Box 481, Loveland, CO 80539.

Christian Growth

Why This Meeting Is Important

Some teenagers don't understand that when they or their friends become Christians, they've just crossed the *starting line,* not the finish line. They've experienced a new birth that will bring hopes, struggles, failures, and successes. Use this meeting to help your teenagers explore what it means to grow in the Christian life.

What Students Will Learn

In this meeting junior highers will
- discover that becoming a Christian is the *beginning* of a new life,
- go on a "faith walk" to discover aspects of the Christian life, and
- commit to pursue a Christlike quality in the coming week.

Before the Meeting

Read the meeting, and gather supplies. Write the words, "righteousness," "godliness," "faith," "love," "endurance," and "gentleness" on separate sheets of newsprint, and post the signs around the room. Also plan a walk around your church grounds with four different spots where teenagers can stop, read their Bibles, and respond to questions on their "Journey Cards" handouts.

Supplies

You'll need Bibles, a marker, newsprint, tape, scissors, and photocopies of the "Journey Cards" handout (p. 25).

Additional supplies for optional activities: newspaper; a wastebasket; a recipe, ingredients, and supplies to make cookies—including an oven; Bibles with concordances; markers; and index cards.

THEMES

Faith, Personal Character, Spiritual Growth

SCRIPTURE

Romans 7:15-25; 8:5-17;
1 Corinthians 9:24-26;
2 Corinthians 3:17-18;
1 Thessalonians 3:12-13;
1 Thessalonians 5:23-24;
1 Timothy 6:11;
2 Timothy 4:7-8;
Hebrews 12:1-12

Choose Your Opener

Opener Option 1: Practice Almost Makes Perfect

You'll need newspaper and a wastebasket.

Set the wastebasket in the center of the room. As teenagers arrive, have them wad the newspaper and shoot baskets into the wastebasket. Say: **Go ahead and shoot a few baskets. Take your time and warm up. Challenge the people around you to a trick shot or two.** After everyone's arrived, ask:

- How did practicing help you shoot better shots?
- Did you get better after you had time to practice?
- Would you become perfect at shooting baskets if you practiced a lot?
- What else have you done that's required time and practice to get better?
- How is that like or unlike the way we grow and mature as Christians?

Say: **Today we're going to take a look at how we grow as Christians.**

Opener Option 2: Recipe for the Christian Life

You'll need a recipe, ingredients, and cooking supplies to make cookies—including an oven; tape; a sheet of newsprint; and a marker.

After teenagers arrive, have them form as many groups as there are ingredients in the cookie recipe. Assign each group a certain ingredient; then have teenagers make the cookies, adding the groups' ingredients at the proper time.

Afterward, when the students are enjoying the cookies, ask:

- What was necessary for these cookies to turn out just right?
- Why was the recipe important? the baking time?

Tape a sheet of newsprint to a wall, and ask:

- If you had to write a "recipe" for growth in our Christian life, what would you include?

Write students' responses on the newsprint, then say: **Today we're going to take a look at how we grow as Christians.**

Bible Experience: Faith Journey

You'll need Bibles, scissors, and photocopies of the "Journey Cards" handout (p. 25).

Say: **We're going to go on a journey to symbolize our Christian walk. I'm going to distribute journey cards that you'll need to complete on our journey. We're going to stop at different spots along the way to find out what's involved in our growth as Christians.** Give each student a Bible and a journey card from the "Journey Cards" handout, and then say:

LEADER TIP

If you have time, enlarge the journey cards when you make photocopies. Then make the cards into "backstage pass" necklaces. Punch a hole in the top of each card, laminate it, and lace a string or ribbon through the hole and tie a knot.

Let's get started. Our first stop is this starting line. Designate a starting line at the door of the room. Have students begin with "Stop 1" on their cards.

Lead students through the course, having them answer the questions on their journey cards. When they finish the journey, ask:

- **Which of the stops on our journey could you most identify with?**
- **What did you learn about Christian growth from our journey?**

Then read 2 Timothy 4:7-8, and say: **You'll notice we didn't cross a finish line at the end of our journey. Where is our finish line?**

Reflection: The Ongoing Process

You'll need a Bible and the newsprint sheets of characteristics you taped up around the room before the meeting.

Read aloud 1 Timothy 6:11. Say: **Paul challenges us to pursue all the qualities on these signs. That means these things cannot be obtained all at once. God is growing these things within us, and it takes time. As a goal this week, choose one of these characteristics to pursue and an action that will help you pursue it. For example, for gentleness, you might pledge to not yell at your brother or sister. For righteousness, you might pledge to compliment someone this week rather than putting someone down. I'm going to ask you to stand, raise your hand, and complete the phrase, "To pursue [fill in the blank], I'll..."** After teenagers have created and declared their pledges for the week, read aloud 1 Thessalonians 3:12-13 as a prayer.

Choose Your Closing

Closing Option 1: He Will Do It

You'll need the newsprint signs from the "Reflection: The Ongoing Process" activity.

Indicate the newsprint signs, and say: **All of us have room to grow in one of these six areas. Move to the sign that represents an area you know will be a challenge this week. Then quietly pray for yourself and for those who are in your group that this week you may grow in this area of your Christian life.** After students have finished praying, read 1 Thessalonians 5:23-24.

Closing Option 2: Encouraging Words

You'll need Bibles with concordances, markers, index cards, and the sheets of newsprint from the "Reflection: The Ongoing Process" activity.

Have teenagers get into six groups. Distribute Bibles and markers. Have

EXTRA! EXTRA!

Try this low-maintenance activity: Buy some frog eggs at a pet store or a teachers supply store. By watching the week-to-week changes in your frog eggs (from eggs to tadpoles to frogs), you can revisit this lesson and discuss the process of growing in our Christian life.

each group move to one of the six newsprint signs. Say: **Each of these characteristics represents an area we can grow in as Christians. In your groups, look up the word on your sign in the concordance in the back of your Bibles to find verses that talk about our Christian growth. Write the Bible references on the newsprint signs. Find at least three verses related to your word.** After teenagers have finished, read aloud 1 Thessalonians 5:23-24.

Journey Cards

Cut apart these cards, and distribute them to students.

Journey Card

 Read 1 Corinthians 9:24-26, and discuss these questions with a partner:
- Why do you think becoming a Christian is considered the starting line rather than the finish line?
- Why do you think Paul uses imagery of a race for the Christian life?

 Read Romans 7:15-25, and discuss these questions with a partner:
- When have you experienced the struggle Paul writes about?
- What do you do when you're caught in this struggle?

 Read Romans 8:5-17 and 2 Corinthians 3:17-18, and discuss this question with a new partner:
- What kind of hope do these verses give you in regard to struggling with sin?

 Read Hebrews 12:1-12, and discuss these questions with a new partner:
- When have you experienced "discipline" from God?
- What was the outcome?

 Discuss this question with a new partner:
- What are some things that can strengthen us in our Christian walk or help us "run the race" well?

Journey Card

 Read 1 Corinthians 9:24-26, and discuss these questions with a partner:
- Why do you think becoming a Christian is considered the starting line rather than the finish line?
- Why do you think Paul uses imagery of a race for the Christian life?

 Read Romans 7:15-25, and discuss these questions with a partner:
- When have you experienced the struggle Paul writes about?
- What do you do when you're caught in this struggle?

 Read Romans 8:5-17 and 2 Corinthians 3:17-18, and discuss this question with a new partner:
- What kind of hope do these verses give you in regard to struggling with sin?

 Read Hebrews 12:1-12, and discuss these questions with a new partner:
- When have you experienced "discipline" from God?
- What was the outcome?

 Discuss this question with a new partner:
- What are some things that can strengthen us in our Christian walk or help us "run the race" well?

Permission to photocopy this handout from *High-Energy Meetings for Young Teenagers* granted for local church use. Copyright © Group Publishing, Inc., P.O. Box 481, Loveland, CO 80539.

The Forgiving Father

THEMES

Forgiveness, God, Love

SCRIPTURE

Luke 15:11-24;
Romans 8:35-39

Why This Meeting Is Important

Junior highers hear—and see—many definitions of the word "love." This meeting will help them experience and understand God's definition of love: selfless giving as demonstrated by a forgiving father who welcomes home a rebellious son.

What Students Will Learn

In this meeting junior highers will

- discover that God offers them a selfless, forgiving love;
- realize that nothing can separate them from God's love; and
- brainstorm ways to live out God's faithful love.

Before the Meeting

Read the meeting, and gather supplies. If you choose the "Decisions, Decisions" opener, write the following questions on a sheet of newsprint, and tape the newsprint to a wall:

- "What would you do if this money were real?"
- "Would you spend it? How? Would you save it? Why?"
- "How long do you think your money would last?"
- "What would your parents think of your money decisions?"

Supplies

You'll need Bibles, pencils, and a selection of blank postcards.

Additional supplies for optional activities: a marker, newsprint, tape, Monopoly money or fake money, newspapers, magazines, scissors, glue, pieces of cardboard, a small prize, and colorful tissue paper.

Choose Your Opener

Opener Option 1: Decisions, Decisions

You'll need Monopoly money or fake money and the questions you wrote on newsprint before the meeting.

As students arrive, give each person $100,000 in Monopoly money or fake money. Have students form trios and discuss the questions you wrote on newsprint before the meeting.

After a few minutes, have trios share their responses with the whole group. Say: **Jesus told a story about a man who didn't make good decisions in his life, yet his father responded in a remarkable way. Let's take a look at that story.**

Opener Option 2: Life Just Ain't Fair

You'll need newspapers, magazines, scissors, glue, a piece of cardboard for each trio, and a small prize.

Have teenagers form trios. Hand out old newspapers and magazines along with scissors, glue, and a piece of cardboard for each group. Ask trios to create collages of words, headlines, and pictures that prove "life just ain't fair"—pictures of beautiful models; success stories; and headlines about crime victims, poverty, or famine, for example.

Allow enough time for teenagers to finish their collages, and then ask trios to share and explain their artwork. Have teenagers vote on the best collage, but give a prize to the group with the collage that received the least number of votes. Allow teenagers to boo, hiss, and express their displeasure. Ask:

- **How did you feel when I gave the prize to the group that didn't get the votes?**
- **How is that like or unlike real life?**
- **How do you normally react when things don't seem fair?**

Say: **Today we'll look at a story Jesus told about a family in which things just weren't fair. At least, that's what *one* of two brothers thought.**

Bible Experience: Over the Line

You'll need Bibles.

Ask:

- **What would it take for your parents to disown you?**
- **What would happen if you spray-painted the school? stole a car? murdered a sister or brother?**
- **Do you know anyone who's ever been disowned?**

- Have you ever disowned anyone?
- What causes someone to disown another person?

Have trios read Luke 15:11-24 together. Ask:

- What were the younger brother's crimes?
- How did his father react?
- Why do you think he reacted this way?
- How does this story mirror or not mirror God's love for us?
- Is it hard for you to imagine someone loving you this much? Why or why not?
- What will it take for God to disown us?
- Is there anything that can separate us from God's love?

Read Romans 8:35-39. Ask:

- How can this Scripture passage affect how we live our lives each day?

Reflection: Postcards Home

You'll need pencils and a selection of blank postcards.

Give each person three postcards and a pencil. Say: **Pretend you're the younger brother in the story. You're going to write two postcards home to Dad: one from the big city while you're still rich and having fun, and the second from the pig farm when things aren't going so great.**

After a few minutes, collect the postcards and shuffle them. Say: **You were just the younger brother, but now pretend you're the father. Your son has run away from home to live a dangerous, foolish life. You want what's best for him. What would that be?** Have students offer suggestions.

Then ask:

- Do any of these postcards show what's best for your son?

Read some of the postcards. Ask:

- How did it feel to hear these postcards from the son you love?
- What did you feel like doing to or for your son when you heard how he was living?
- Would your actions match what the father really did in the story from Scripture?
- Why do you think the father acted as he did?
- What do you think was going on inside the younger brother to allow him to make the decision to go home?

Say: **Let's write a postcard to God, our loving Father. Your postcards won't be collected or read. Spend a few quiet moments thinking about whether you're running away from God in any way. Then talk to God about it. Finally, thank God for his patience with us and the way he welcomes home runaways.**

LEADER TIP

Encourage students to send postcards to their parents, friends, or relatives reminding them of how much God loves them.

Choose Your Closing

Closing Option 1: Forgiving Love

You'll need colorful tissue paper and tape.

Distribute the tissue paper and tape, and have teenagers make rings they can wear on their fingers.

Say: **A good title for the parable we've just looked at might be the Parable of the Forgiving Father. God's love is a forgiving, caring love— even for those who've treated God poorly in the past.**

Have teenagers find partners. Say: **With your partner, pray for at least one person who's treated you poorly either in the past or in the present. Make sure both partners get to pray. Then brainstorm about how you might express God's forgiving love to the people you've prayed for.**

After you're done, exchange rings with your partner as a pledge to pray for your partner during the coming week. Pray that he or she will be able to express God's love to the person who's wronged him or her.

Closing Option 2: Unconditional Love

You'll need Bibles.

In pairs have teenagers take turns reading aloud Luke 15:20-24 to one another, each ending with the words, "God loves you no matter what." Then gather for a group hug and a quick prayer of thanks.

Givers and Takers

THEMES

Purpose, Service

SCRIPTURE

Matthew 25:31-46;
John 15:12-13

Why This Meeting Is Important

In a self-centered world, it's easy for us to forget about serving others. However, God wants Christians not to be selfish and lifeless but alive in deed to those in need. Use this meeting to help teenagers look beyond themselves and reach out to others.

What Students Will Learn

In this meeting junior highers will

- experience giving and taking,
- discover God's will for serving others, and
- affirm teenagers' positive "servant" traits and abilities.

Before the Meeting

Read the meeting, and gather supplies.

Supplies

You'll need Bibles, newsprint, markers, tape, nails, and glue.
Additional supplies for optional activities: index cards, pennies, and pencils.

Choose Your Opener

Opener Option 1: Give or Take

You'll need three index cards and a penny for each person.

Give each student three index cards and a penny. Have students form pairs. Have the oldest person in each pair toss the penny and call "heads" or "tails." If the coin lands the way the person called it, the person wins the toss and must give one of his or her cards to the other person. Then have teenagers find new partners and repeat the process. Play the game until one person gives away all of his or her cards. Then ask:

- Which was more fun in this game: giving or taking? Why?
- Is giving or taking more important to the Christian faith? Why?
- How did you feel when you received cards? when you gave cards away?

Say: Our Christian faith is built upon the idea of giving. "For God so loved the world that he gave his one and only Son" (John 3:16a). Yet we live in a world that often is more concerned with taking than giving. But Jesus showed us it's more important to give than to take. Let's find out more about giving.

Opener Option 2: I Want That

Have students form pairs. Say: One person at a time, take one item of your choice from your partner, such as a watch, ring, or pencil. The oldest partner goes first. Then the second partner may select one item from the first, but you can't retrieve the item you've just lost!

Allow time for the exchange, and then have teenagers form new pairs. Say: Now give an item of your choice to your partner. The item you give away must not be the item you just took from another person. The older partner goes first, then the younger partner.

After the exchange ask:
- Which was easier to do: take something from another person or give something? Why?
- How did you decide which item to give to another person?
- Which is most important in Christian life: giving or taking? Why?

Have teenagers return items to their original owners. Say: It's difficult to give up something of value, isn't it? But it sure can be easy to take. Unfortunately, we live in a world more concerned with taking than giving. The Bible teaches that we should strive daily to give to those in need. Let's find out more about giving.

Bible Experience: Those Sheep and Goats

You'll need Bibles, newsprint, markers, and tape.

Have students form groups of no more than three. Give each group a Bible, sheet of newsprint, a marker, and one of the following descriptions: "hungry or thirsty," "stranger or without clothes," "sick or in prison." It's OK if more than one group is assigned the same description. Have each group choose a reader who will read Matthew 25:31-46, a recorder who will write ideas on the newsprint, and a reporter who will tell the ideas to the whole group.

Have groups identify actual people in their community who fit their descriptions and then list ways to serve these people. For example, groups could write, "Poor or unemployed people: Collect canned and

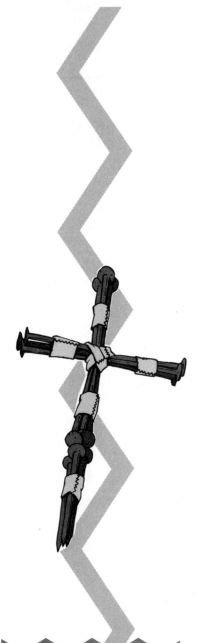

packaged food for them"; "Homeless people: Collect money and clothing for them"; or "People in nursing homes, hospitals, or prisons: Send cards and letters to them."

After several minutes, have each group's reporter share the group's ideas. Post the newsprint lists on a wall. Then ask:

- Why is it important to give to those in need?
- What earthly rewards do we receive from our willingness to help?
- What heavenly rewards might we inherit?

Say: **Jesus says that unless we love the "least of these," we can't truly love him. God wants Christians not to be selfish and lifeless, but alive in deed to those in need.**

Reflection: Greater Love

You'll need a Bible, nails, glue, and tape.

Give each person a nail. Ask teenagers to hold their nails as tightly as possible while you read aloud John 15:12-13. Ask:

- How did your hand feel as you held your nail?
- How is that like following Jesus' command to love others?
- Why is reaching out in love sometimes painful?

Give teenagers glue and tape, and ask them to form a sculpture with the nails to symbolize the passage. For example, students could create a cross or heart shape.

Say: **God wants us to show our love for others by giving of ourselves and helping them. Turn to a person sitting close to you and say one way you'll reach out to another person this week. It might be any idea listed on the sheets of newsprint. It might be calling a friend to encourage him or her before a test. Or it might be listening to a brother or sister talk about a family problem.**

Allow time for pairs to share. Then pray, asking for God's help as teenagers give of themselves during the upcoming week.

Choose Your Closing

Closing Option 1: Giving Partners

You'll need index cards and pencils.

Have students form pairs. Say: **Let's take some time to affirm one another and our "giver" abilities. Say one way you see your partner serving others through a personal desire or ability. For example, you could say, "Susan, you're such a caring and adventurous person. You'd make a great missionary!"**

LEADER TIP

Have teenagers glue the nail sculpture to a piece of poster board. Display the sculpture in the room as a reminder to give to others just as God gave his Son to us.

After partners have affirmed each other, give each person an index card and pencil. Have teenagers each write a prayer asking God to give them strength, courage, and wisdom to be givers throughout their lives. In pairs have each person read aloud his or her written prayer.

Closing Option 2: Group Givers

You'll need the newsprint lists from the "Bible Experience: Those Sheep and Goats" activity.

Have your teenagers select one "giver" idea from the newsprint lists that they can plan right now. For example, they could plan to collect clothing for homeless families.

Brainstorm about the steps they would need to do to accomplish the task, and then do them. For example, have students form three groups. Have one group write an announcement for your church bulletin or newsletter saying that your group is sponsoring a clothing drive for homeless families. In the announcement, tell congregation members the date to bring blankets, coats, gloves, pants, shirts, and socks to the church. Have another group search the church for boxes to decorate to hold the collected clothing. Have another group look in the phone book for shelters or human services agencies to contact about the clothing the group will collect. The group could write a letter to the organizations asking how to deliver the clothing.

Making Jesus the Center of Your Life

THEMES

Choices, Jesus, Priorities, Spiritual Growth

SCRIPTURE

Matthew 6:24, 33; Mark 12:30; Philippians 3:7-11

LEADER TIP

Teenagers learn by observing adults' behavior, so "walk your talk." Tell teenagers about your insights, and be enthusiastic about your church experiences. *Show* that Jesus is the center of your life.

Why This Meeting Is Important

Hobbies, possessions, skills, friends—many things compete for the number one spot in our lives. But Jesus wants to be in that number one spot. He wants to get our focus off worldly priorities and onto him, because if Christ lives in our hearts by faith, our lives will be strong in love (Ephesians 3:17).

Use this meeting to help teenagers focus on Jesus and make him the center of their lives.

What Students Will Learn

In this meeting junior highers will

- examine what the Bible says about making Christ the center of their lives,
- discuss things that compete with Christ for control, and
- reaffirm Christ as the center of their lives.

Before the Meeting

Read the meeting, and gather supplies.

Supplies

You'll need Bibles, paper, and pencils.

Additional supplies for optional activities: index cards, pens, and nice paper such as parchment paper or document paper.

Choose Your Opener

Opener Option 1: Master for a Minute

Welcome teenagers, and have them form groups of no more than six. Choose one person in each group to be the master. Say: **The person I've** chosen in your group is your master. The rest of you are slaves. On "go," masters will command their slaves to do whatever they want. For example, masters can command slaves to do jumping jacks or walk around and quack like ducks. Masters can't ask slaves to do anything rude or gross, and slaves must obey the commands. I'll circulate among the groups to make sure everyone is obeying. Ready? Go!

After masters have reigned for one minute, call time. Switch roles so others can experience being masters and slaves. Afterward ask:

- How did you feel when you were a master? a slave?
- What "masters" do we follow in real life? How do these masters make us act?

Say: The Bible says we're going to be slaves to something or someone. This may come as a surprise to you, but you can choose who will be your master. Let's talk about the greatest master of our lives—Jesus.

Opener Option 2: The Control Tower Tragedy

Welcome teenagers, and give each one a part in a drama. You'll need one control captain, four renegade air controllers, four pilots, and four copilots. The rest of the teenagers are people in the terminal. Increase or decrease the parts, depending on the number of teenagers. Have each pilot and copilot pair link arms to represent an airplane.

Explain that the setting is a busy airport. Use your entire room as the stage. Have the actors act out their parts as you read aloud this story:

Once upon a time at a busy airport, four renegade air controllers did not want to listen to their control captain. The renegade air controllers plugged their ears. Then they carried the control captain to a corner and made him sit there. The renegade air controllers marched out to the four corners of the airfield. Each of them set up their own control area. They began yelling at four airplanes that were buzzing and flying around the airport. The pilots and copilots couldn't figure out where to land so they circled round and round the airport. The renegade air controllers began to wave their arms. This made the planes go round and round faster. This made the pilots and copilots throw up on each other. The planes turned sharply. This made the pilots and copilots fall all over each other. The renegade air controllers shouted even louder. By now the planes were running out of fuel. One plane crashed and rolled across the runway. One plane crashed into the people in the terminal. The people in the terminal screamed. One plane landed safely, but then the last plane landed on top of it. The end.

Have everyone sit down. Ask:

- How did you feel acting out the story?
- Who was in control of the planes?

- Why is one central control captain essential for air traffic safety?
- Who or what controls your life?
- How is Jesus like a central control captain?

Say: Today we're going to talk about the one greatest control captain in our lives—Jesus.

Bible Experience: Help Wanted

You'll need Bibles, paper, and pencils.

Have students form four groups. Give each group a Bible, a sheet of paper, and a pencil. Assign each group one of these verses: Matthew 6:24; 6:33; Mark 12:30; Philippians 3:7-11.

Say: Imagine that God has employed your group to write a help wanted ad for the Heavenly Times newspaper. God is searching for true servants of Christ, people who will make Jesus the center of their lives. Read your passage, and then write your ad. For example, you could write, "Help wanted: Need a true servant of Christ who is willing to love and serve only God." List all the requirements you can find in your passage.

After five minutes, have representatives from each group read their Heavenly Times ads. Ask:

- What do you think it takes to make Jesus the center of your life?
- What difference does it make when we make Jesus the center of our lives?

LEADER TIP

Post the help wanted ads in your classroom to remind teenagers to keep Christ in the center of their lives.

Reflection: Center Stage

Say: We've heard what the Bible says about giving Jesus the number one spot in our lives, but we often let other things fill that spot. In your groups, discuss things that compete for control in your lives. These are not necessarily bad things but merely things that can easily take priority—sports and friends, for example. Choose one idea, and then create a quick skit to represent that idea. For example, you could show off fancy clothes or wild possessions.

Clear the front of the room to use as a stage. After five minutes, have groups present their quick skits.

Choose Your Closing

Closing Option 1: Dead Center

You'll need index cards and pencils.

Give each student an index card and a pencil. Say: **Many things compete** for control of our lives. At the top of your card, write one thing you tend to make the center of your life rather than Christ.

Have students form pairs. Have partners share what they've written. Next have students each write a prayer on their cards, asking Jesus to be the center of their lives. Have partners pray about what they've written on their cards. Have teenagers take home their cards as reminders to keep Jesus in the center of their lives.

Closing Option 2: Covenants

You'll need pens and nice paper such as parchment paper or document paper.

Give each person a pen and a sheet of nice paper. Say: **Many things compete for control of our lives. Let's recommit to making Christ the center of our lives. On your sheet of paper, write a covenant, or promise, to Jesus about making him the master of your life. Sign your covenant to symbolize your commitment.**

Have students read their covenants to each other. Then allow time for all students to sign each other's covenants as witnesses.

Mustard Seed Faith

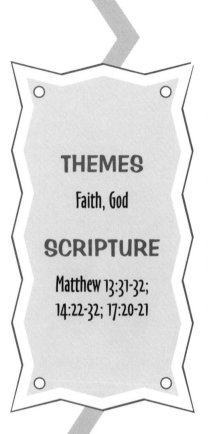

THEMES

Faith, God

SCRIPTURE

Matthew 13:31-32;
14:22-32; 17:20-21

Why This Meeting Is Important

Often life is an uncomfortable fit for junior highers. They're treated like children one moment and adults the next. They wish they had more to offer and are excruciatingly aware of their shortcomings.

This meeting will help junior highers see that God can do remarkable things with very little—and that with faith, God can do great things through them.

What Students Will Learn

In this meeting junior highers will

- learn that God is powerful and can do impossible things,
- examine what keeps them from having more faith, and
- pray for each other to grow in faith.

Before the Meeting

Read the meeting, and gather supplies. If you choose the "Dash of Salt" opener, be sure to wash your hands before placing salt on students' tongues.

Supplies

You'll need Bibles, newsprint, tape, and a marker.

Additional supplies for optional activities: salt, a three-foot piece of rope or twine for each group of three students, and flower seeds.

Choose Your Opener

Opener Option 1: A Dash of Salt

You'll need salt.

As teenagers arrive, ask them to participate in a taste test. Have them close their eyes, and then place a small dash of salt on their tongues. Ask:

- **What do you taste?**

- How much salt did I place on your tongue?
- How much salt does it take to make a difference on your food?
- How is that like or unlike the amount of faith it takes to make a difference?

Say: **Jesus said it takes only a little faith to make a big difference. Let's find out what Jesus meant.**

Opener Option 2: Desert Island

You'll need a three-foot piece of rope or twine for each group of three people.

Ask teenagers to form trios. Give each trio a three-foot piece of rope or twine. Say: **I've got some bad news. You're stranded on a desert island. But here's the good news: There are coconut trees, a natural spring, and plenty of fish out in the lagoon—*and* one person in your group grabbed this rope as your boat sank. You need to think of ways the rope can help your group survive. You have three minutes to come up with as many ideas as possible. Go!**

After three minutes, collect the ropes, and ask trios to share their ideas with the whole group. When everyone's finished, say: **Now let's pretend that someone in your group has matches in his or her pocket. You have one minute to think of ways those matches can help you survive. Go!**

After a minute, have groups report their ideas. Then say: **Great ideas, but there's a problem. The person with the matches has decided they're not important. He or she doesn't mention them. It turns out you don't even *know* about them. How many of your ideas will work if the matches aren't available?**

Say: **You've proven you can do a lot with very little—*if* it's yours to use. And God can do infinitely *more* with very little—*if* we make ourselves available to him.**

Bible Experience: "Impossible" Things

You'll need Bibles, newsprint, tape, and a marker.

Distribute Bibles, and have teenagers read aloud Matthew 17:20-21 together. Tape a sheet of newsprint to a wall, and say: **Let's brainstorm about "impossible" things God has done in Scripture.** Write students' ideas on the newsprint. Afterward ask:

- **Why would God do these impossible things?**
- **Was there someone in each of these situations who had faith in God? Who?** (Have teenagers look up Scriptures if they can't remember.)

Record students' comments on the newsprint. Then say: **Now brainstorm a second list: impossible things you would like God to do in *your* life.** Afterward ask:

LEADER TIP

When teenagers are in groups brainstorming or discussing, give two-minute, one-minute, and thirty-second warnings as time passes. You'll help students pace themselves so they're ready when you suddenly whistle or flip the light switch to close the brainstorming exercise.

- Why would God do these things?
- Is there someone with faith in each of these situations? Who?

Reflection: Help! I'm Sinking!

You'll need Bibles.

Ask teenagers to form pairs. Have pairs read Matthew 14:22-32. Ask:

- What was impossible about what Peter wanted to do?
- Why couldn't he do it?

Say: **In your pairs, talk about what keeps you from believing God can do the impossible things on our list. Then think about how you can encourage your partner to believe and have faith that God can do these things.** After a few minutes, have pairs share their ideas with the whole group.

Choose Your Closing

Closing Option 1: Pair Prayer

Have students pray for each other as you lead a directed prayer. Say: **I'm going to suggest things we could pray for. The person in your pair who's wearing the most yellow will pray first. Please pray so only your partner can hear you.**

Pray: **God, hear us as we pray to grow in faith.**

Say: **Begin by praising God for his awesome power.** Pause. **Thank God for the many impossible things he has done.** Pause. **Thank God for the things he has yet to do.** Pause. **Ask God to help us replace our doubt with faith.**

Have partners switch so the other person gets to pray. Lead the directed prayer again.

Closing Option 2: Seed Prayer

You'll need a Bible for each group and a flower seed for each person.

Ask students to form groups of three, and give each person one flower seed. Say: **The person sitting closest to me is the prayer leader for your group. Listen quietly as your prayer leader reads Matthew 13:31-32 and 17:20-21. Hold your seed for two minutes while you think about one area in your life where even a little faith can make a difference—at home, at school, or in a friendship, for example. Then when I signal, go around the circle, beginning with the prayer leader, and say a prayer asking God to help you live out your faith day by day.**

What's God's Purpose for Me?

Why This Meeting Is Important

Junior highers are asking questions such as "Who am I?" and "What will I be?" Use this meeting to help kids see that God has already given them a wealth of information in his Word about who he wants them to be.

What Students Will Learn

In this meeting junior highers will

- think about what God desires for their lives,
- learn from God's Word what his purposes are for us, and
- hear stories of God's purpose and direction in the lives of "veteran" Christians.

Before the Meeting

Read the meeting, and gather supplies. Ask an adult volunteer to help you with the "Bible Experience: God's Will Already Revealed" activity. On a sheet of newsprint, write the following Scripture references and discussion questions:

- "Exodus 20:1-17; Mark 12:30-31; Romans 13:3-10; James 1:22–2:1; 1 John 4:7-21"
- "How did these verses help you understand God's will for you?"
- "How could these verses help you in specific situations in which you're wondering what God's will is for you—for example, if you're wondering whether to be friends with someone or whether to obey your parents?"
- "What good could come to us from obeying God's will as it's already revealed in his Word?"

If you choose the "Differing Desires" opener, write the words, "Parent," "Teachers," "Youth Pastor," and "God" on separate sheets of newsprint and tape them in different corners of your meeting area. If you choose the "Tell Me a Story" closing, invite several older members of your congregation to come to the meeting and share with your group how they've experienced God's will and purpose for their lives over the years.

THEMES

Bible, God, Purpose

SCRIPTURE

Exodus 20:1-17;
Mark 12:30-31;
Romans 13:3-10;
James 1:5-6, 22–2:1;
1 Peter 2:4-5;
1 John 4:7-21

Supplies

You'll need Bibles, newsprint, and a marker.

Additional supplies for optional activities: photocopies of the "Going to the Source" handout (p. 45), colorful markers, and tape.

Choose Your Opener

Opener Option 1: Going to the Source

You'll need two photocopies of the "Going to the Source" handout (p. 45).

Give photocopies of the skit to two junior highers. Have the rest of the group gather around them as they perform the skit. Afterward ask:

- How was this skit like how we seek or don't seek God's direction in our lives?
- What might the instruction book in the skit represent?
- Do you think there's any sure way to know what God desires for our lives?

Say: If we're curious about God's purpose for our lives, it makes sense to begin looking at what he's already given us—his Word. Let's do that now.

Opener Option 2: Differing Desires

You'll need markers and the newsprint signs you prepared before the meeting.

Distribute the markers, and ask:

- Do you have any idea what God, your parents, or others want you to be?

Say: I'd like you to write your thoughts on the sheets of newsprint posted around the room according to the person listed at the top.

Have kids travel around the room, writing their thoughts on the newsprint. After a few minutes, read aloud some of the responses. Ask:

- Which of these sheets of newsprint was hardest to fill out and why?

Say: Sometimes it's hard to know exactly what God wants us to do or be. Today we're going to begin to take a look at what God's purposes for us really are.

Bible Experience: God's Will Already Revealed

You'll need Bibles and the Scripture references and questions you wrote on newsprint before the meeting.

Have kids get into groups of four, and distribute Bibles. Have half the groups meet in one area of the room and the other half meet in another area of the room. Give half the groups the following instructions: **Your job** is to find verses in the Bible that show us what God's will is for us. Ready? Go.

Have your volunteer give these instructions and the sheet of newsprint you prepared before the meeting to the other groups: **Your job is to look up two of these verses and then discuss the questions that follow.**

After about fifteen minutes, bring the groups together again. Ask the first set of groups:

- How easy or difficult was this experience?
- How much did you get done?
- How much did you learn?

Ask the second set of groups:

- Were you able to follow the directions you received? Why or why not?
- What did you learn?

Say: **Without clear direction, we can drift and miss out on important truths like those in this activity—and in life. But God has given us specific direction in his Word about who he wants us to be and become. Let's have the second set of groups share with the other groups what they learned about God's will.** Have each group that answered the questions partner with a group that didn't and share what they learned from Scripture.

Reflection: Seeking God

You'll need a Bible.

Have students form pairs. Say: **Think of a time in your life when you needed guidance or direction.** Ask:

- Where did you go for help?
- What was the outcome?

Read aloud James 1:5-6. Say: **Another way we can learn about God's purposes for us is through prayer. Think of one area in your life in which you need guidance and direction. Pray with your partner about that situation, asking God to lead and guide you.**

Choose Your Closing

Closing Option 1: Tell Me a Story

You'll need volunteers from your congregation to share their experiences.

Say: **Paul Little said in his booklet "Affirming the Will of God" that the will of God for our lives is more like a scroll that unrolls each day rather than a "magic package" that falls from the sky. I've invited some members of our congregation to our meeting to tell us about how** they've experienced God's will and purpose for them and how they saw his plan unfold. Let's listen.

After volunteers have shared, close the meeting in prayer.

Closing Option 2: God's Workmanship

You'll need a Bible, newsprint, and colorful markers.

Spread out the newsprint, and set out the markers. Have students spread around the perimeter of the paper. Say: **Little by little, God is building you into who he wants you to be. On the section of paper in front of you, please draw a house or dwelling that looks like something you'd like to live in one day. Leave a large area inside the house open because we'll be writing inside it later.**

After students have finished drawing, say: **Now write one thing that shows how God has led you in some area of your life—by guiding you to this group or by answering a prayer, for example.**

After students have finished writing, say: **Now we're going to move around the paper, writing in each other's houses ways in which we see God building us into who he wants us to be. For example, you might write that God's given Craig an ability to make people laugh. Let's start moving to the right.**

After teenagers have finished, close by reading 1 Peter 2:4-5 as a prayer.

Going to the Source

SETTING: Teenagers are doing homework either at a table or on the floor.

FRIEND 1: Gosh, this math is driving me nuts! I just can't figure it out!

FRIEND 2: Well, here's the instruction book. Remember, the teacher said it was OK to look in here when we had questions.

FRIEND 1: Nah. Who wants to take time with that? Let's just call Toby. He's good at this stuff. Or we could look at my brother's high school textbook. Maybe there are some answers in there.

FRIEND 2: I don't know…

FRIEND 1: Yeah. Let's do that. And if that doesn't work, I think there's a hotline we can call. And there's also a math Web site we can check out.

FRIEND 2: *Shakes head and looks at instruction book.*

Permission to photocopy this handout from *High-Energy Meetings for Young Teenagers* granted for local church use.
Copyright © Group Publishing, Inc., P.O. Box 481, Loveland, CO 80539.

Section 2

GROWING UP

Bible Heroes
Who Blew It

Why This Meeting Is Important

Have you ever failed so badly at something that you thought God wouldn't want anything to do with you anymore? A lot of junior highers have. They think God doesn't want them anymore.

But there's good news: God wants you and them no matter what! Throughout Scripture, God has shown his patience and love for people—even when they fail. Use this meeting to help your teenagers understand that if they only turn back to God, he will pick them up and get them going again after they've blown it.

What Students Will Learn

In this meeting junior highers will

* experience how it feels to get a second chance,
* learn from people in the Bible who blew it, and
* consider how their own response to failure can affect their future.

Before the Meeting

Read the meeting, and gather supplies.

Supplies

You'll need Bibles, pencils, and paper.
Additional supplies for optional activities: a small foam ball.

Choose Your Opener

Opener Option 1: Second-Chance Quiz

You'll need paper and pencils.

Distribute paper and pencils, and then read aloud the "Bible Quiz" from the box on the following page. Have students write their answers on their papers. Don't allow students to use Bibles or other source materials.

THEMES

Bible, Failure, Forgiveness, God

SCRIPTURE

Mark 10:17-22; 14:66-72; 17:22; Acts 2:14-24; 4:8-20; 7:54—8:3; 9:1-20; 20:17-24

When you've finished the quiz, have students correct their papers as you give the answers. Then say: **Some of you probably didn't do so well on that quiz. I'm going to give you another chance.**

Distribute paper again, and give students the same quiz. After you've gone over the answers again, say: **Let's not count that first quiz. Let's just throw those first quizzes away and keep the second quizzes.** Ask:

- How did you feel when I said we'd forget the first quiz?
- How is that similar to or different from the way God treats us?

Say: **God gives us second chances. The Bible is full of stories about imperfect people God never gave up on. The questions on this quiz relate to some of those people. We're going to take a closer look at these people and see how God reacted to people who blew it.**

 BIBLE QUIZ

1. What Bible book tells about a rich young man who asked Jesus a question? (Matthew, Mark, or Luke)
2. Who was preaching when Lydia responded to the Lord? (Paul)
3. Who held the coats as Stephen was stoned? (Paul)
4. Who preached a long sermon on the day of Pentecost? (Peter)
5. What disciple did the angels mention by name after Jesus had risen from the dead? (Peter)

Opener Option 2: The Catch

You'll need a small foam ball.

Say: **I'm going to toss this ball to someone, and it's very important that you catch it.**

Toss the ball to someone but make it a bit difficult to catch. If the person doesn't catch the ball, toss it to that person again until he or she catches it. Have the person toss it back to you. Then toss it to someone else. If you have time, toss the ball until everyone in your group catches it. Be sure you toss the ball so at least several people don't catch it the first time you throw it. Ask:

- How did you feel when you missed a catch?
- How did you feel when I gave you another chance to catch the ball?
- How is this similar to or different from the way God treats us?

LEADER TIP

Use caution and consider your students' personalities when you throw the ball. For example, you probably don't want to zing a fastball at a student who's sensitive about his or her physical abilities or who others tease about being unathletic.

Say: God gives us second chances when we mess up. And today we're going to look at people in the Bible who failed. We'll see how God gave them second chances.

Bible Experience: Three Who Blew It

You'll need Bibles, pencils, and paper.

Have students form three groups. Say: **Peter, Paul, and a rich young man are all people in the Bible who messed up. Let's take a closer look at these three.** Assign each group one of the Bible characters. Say: **You have one minute to find in the Bible where your person messed up and to jot down what he did wrong. Go.**

After one minute call time, and have groups report. Then say: **I think you could do better with a second chance.** Tell the rich-young-man group to look in Mark 10:17-22; the Peter group to look in Mark 14:66-72; and the Paul (also called Saul) group to look in Acts 7:54–8:3. After groups read their passages, have them explain what their person did wrong. Ask:

- How did you feel when I gave you a second chance to find the information?
- How is this similar to or different from the way God deals with us?
- How does God want us to respond to the second chances he gives us?

Say: **God realizes that we sin and make mistakes. He wants us to turn back to him when we fail, and he wants us to learn from our failures.**

Reflection: Two Who Turned

You'll need Bibles.

Read aloud Mark 17:22, and say: **The rich young man turned away from Jesus and never came back. But Peter and Paul didn't walk away from God. Let's learn how they responded to failure.**

Have students form pairs, and assign each pair one of the following passages: Acts 2:14-24; 4:8-20; 9:1-20; 20:17-24. Have students discover from their passages how Peter and Paul responded to the second chances God gave them. After about five minutes, have pairs report their findings. Then ask:

- What was the difference between the way the rich young man responded and the way Peter and Paul responded?
- What difference did their responses make to their futures?
- How does God want us to respond when we fail?
- How can a bad response to failure affect our lives?
- How can a good response to failure affect our lives?

Say: **God is willing to give us a second chance when we fail. And he's willing to help us get up and get on our way in serving him. But God wants us to turn to him when we fail.**

Choose Your Closing

Closing Option 1: Picking up the Ball

You'll need a small foam ball.

Say: If you're like most people, you've already done lots of things that aren't pleasing to God. You may feel like a failure in your faith. But the good news is that God will give you a second chance no matter what you've done. And God can still use you in powerful ways, as he did with Peter and Paul.

Have teenagers form a circle. Say: As we pass around this foam ball, let's each silently commit that if we "drop the ball" when it comes to serving Jesus, we'll pick it up and return to him. Then God will be able to work through us to make a difference in our world.

Hand the ball to someone, and have teenagers silently pass it around. When it gets back to you, end with prayer.

Closing Option 2: For God's Use

Have teenagers return to their pairs from the "Reflection: Two Who Turned" activity. In their pairs have teenagers each tell their partners something they've seen that could indicate how that person could be used by God. Have teenagers encourage each other to take advantage of the second chances God has given them and to serve God faithfully.

Wrap up your meeting with a song such as "More Precious Than Silver" or "By My Spirit." Then close with prayer.

Body Image

THEMES

Friendship, Hot Topics, Personal Character, Self-Image

SCRIPTURE

1 Samuel 16:7

Why This Meeting Is Important

Your junior highers are frequently trying to establish their level of "coolness." Too often, they do this with an all-out attempt to look good. Use this meeting to help kids understand that we can see value in others and in ourselves when we look beyond the packaging.

What Students Will Learn

In this meeting junior highers will
- learn to see through body image to discover one's true identity,
- see what the Bible says about our outward and inward appearance, and
- commit to reaching out to an "ugly duckling."

Before the Meeting

Read the meeting, and gather supplies. Write the following on a sheet of newsprint: "Group 1: adornment, dress, hair, wearing." On a second sheet of newsprint write, "Group 2: character, honest/honesty, truthful, speech."

If you choose the "Photo Shoot" opener, recruit five to ten teenagers to bring "cool" and "nerdy" clothing and accessories and participate in the "field test." Also route a course around the area with masking tape and recruit an adult volunteer.

Supplies

You'll need Bibles, concordances, paper, pencils, marker, newsprint, and four or five products with packaging that either accurately or inaccurately represents the products. Try to select a few packages that do a good job of representing the product and a few that are misleading or plain.

Additional supplies for optional activities: squirt guns or liquid dish-washing bottles filled with water, the "cool" and "nerdy" clothing your junior highers brought, scissors, *paper* shopping bags, masking tape, water-soluble colored markers, and a copy of the Hans Christian Andersen story *The Ugly Duckling*.

Choose Your Opener

Opener Option 1: Photo Shoot

You'll need squirt guns or dishwashing bottles filled with water, the "cool" and "nerdy" clothes your students brought, scissors, and paper shopping bags.

Have the students who brought clothing change into those clothes. Also have them cut out holes for eyes in the paper shopping bags and wear the bags as masks. Have an adult volunteer help these students hide around the course you created. They should hide behind obstacles or in doorways so they can jump out as people approach. Give the other students squirt guns.

Say: **When you're in school, you see many different kinds of people. We've designed a field test to determine if you can quickly identify potential friends. As you walk through the course, people will pop out at you. Shoot them with your squirt guns if you wouldn't want to be close friends with them. Give them high fives if you would want to be close friends with them.**

After the game line up your masked student volunteers, and ask the group who they shot at and why. Then ask:

- **How does this exercise compare with the way you evaluate people at school?**
- **How do you react to the people you see as "uncool"?**
- **What are other ways you can determine if you want to be close friends with someone?**

Opener Option 2: Mirror Image

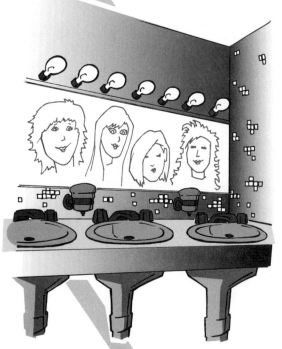

You'll need water-soluble colored markers.

Separate the guys and girls into their respective bathrooms, and give water-soluble colored markers to each group. Give students five minutes to draw self-portraits on the bathroom mirrors. Ask students to be as accurate as possible.

When they've finished, have students switch bathrooms. Have the girls write the names of the guys underneath their drawings, and have the guys do the same with the girls' drawings. See which group correctly identified more portraits. Then bring everyone back together, and ask:

- **What things did you concentrate on to draw an accurate portrait?**
- **What things helped you to identify other people's portraits?**
- **How did it feel to be identified by your outward appearance?**

- Do you think people see you as who you are or as an image? Explain.
- What criteria do you use to choose who your friends are going to be?
- How much does body image play in your decisions?

Bible Experience: Outward vs. Inward Characteristics

You'll need Bibles, concordances, paper, pencils, and the sheets of newsprint you prepared before the meeting.

Say: **Let's look at what the Bible has to say about the importance of our outward and inward appearance.** Have students get into two groups by calling out their birthdays: January through June birthdays in Group 1, and July through December birthdays in Group 2. Distribute Bibles, concordances, paper, pencils, and the sheets of newsprint you prepared before the meeting.

Say: **Use your concordances to look up the list of words on these sheets of newsprint. Group 1, your job is to find verses that help you complete the statement, "The importance of our outward appearance is..." Group 2, your job is to find verses that help you complete the statement, "The importance of our inward appearance is..."** Give students ten to fifteen minutes to use their concordances to find verses and complete their statements. Afterward, have groups take turns reading their verses and sharing their discoveries with the other group. Ask:

- **What did you learn about outward appearance? inward appearance?**
- **Is our outward or inward appearance of more interest to God? Explain.**

Reflection: Proper Packaging

You'll need a Bible and the packages you gathered before the meeting.
Display the packages you brought. Ask:

- **What do these packages communicate to you about what's inside?**

Have teenagers tell about when they've bought things that haven't lived up to the advertising or packaging. Ask:

- **How is your experience with products like or unlike how we judge others by their looks?**
- **Have you ever been surprised at someone's personality after getting to know him or her better?**
- **What outward appearances may not tell us who a person really is?**

Read aloud 1 Samuel 16:7, and say: **Just as God looks inward to learn about a person, we can remember to look inward instead of basing our opinions about a person on outward appearance.**

EXTRA! EXTRA!

1. Damaged Package— Great Product

Invite a mature disabled or visually impaired Christian to speak to your group. Your teenagers can learn that despite outward appearances, they can radiantly reflect Jesus to others.

2. "Prep" Rally

Use this meeting at the beginning of a new school year to welcome the younger students to the group. Plan short seminars on topics such as what to expect in junior high, tips on making good grades, and surviving the teenage years. Invite a Christian teacher, principal, or older students to speak.

Choose Your Closing

Closing Option 1: Getting Your Ducks on the Role

You'll need a copy of the story The Ugly Duckling.

Have teenagers sit on the floor around you. Announce that it's story time. Read aloud *The Ugly Duckling* with great expression. Be sure to show the group the pictures. Afterward ask:

- **What character did you best identify with?**
- **What was it about the ugly duckling's attitude that caused you to like or dislike him?**
- **What do you think the story teaches us about ourselves?**
- **What does the story teach us about others?**

Ask students each to think of at least one person they know who's having a hard time feeling as if they belong. Then ask students each to commit to reaching out to the person they thought of. Close with a prayer, asking God to help students follow through on their commitment and see beyond other people's appearances.

Closing Option 2: What's in My Package?

Ask students to complete this statement: "If I were to see me as I look and dress, I would think…" Encourage teenagers to honestly evaluate if their "outward package" conflicts with the people they want to be inside. Ask:

- **Based on what we've learned, how has your view of yourself or others changed?**

Close with a prayer, asking God to help teenagers accurately reflect the people they want to be on the inside.

Building Confidence

Why This Meeting Is Important

"How can people not like themselves?" asks a nine-year-old boy. By the time that same child turns thirteen, a deep shyness grips him. His confidence plummets. Just when he needs confidence most, it dips dangerously.

Use this meeting to give your junior highers a generous dose of confidence. Help them grow so certain of their value in Christ that they ask, "How can people not like themselves?"

What Students Will Learn

In this meeting junior highers will

- accept a challenge and play a game,
- build others' confidence, and
- discuss why they are important and loved.

THEMES
Confidence, Self-Image

SCRIPTURE
Isaiah 26:1-4;
Philippians 4:4-13

Before the Meeting

Read the meeting, and gather supplies. Write the following "W.H.O." formula on a sheet of newsprint:

Why I matter…

How my actions and attitudes help others know they matter…

One or more skills that help me succeed…

Fill a box with celebration "accessories" such as confetti, ribbons, streamers, balloons, and colored construction paper.

Supplies

You'll need Bibles; a box; celebration accessories such as confetti, ribbons, streamers, balloons, and colored construction paper; index cards; pencils; newsprint; a marker; and tape.

Additional supplies for optional activities: soft, sour candy such as Sour Patch Kids (avoid hard candy because of the choking risk); paper plates; and scissors.

Choose Your Opener

Opener Option 1: Sour Power

You'll need soft, sour candy.

Display some so-sour-I-bet-you-can't-eat-it candy. Have students form teams. Challenge teams each to choose a representative who can eat more sour candy than any other person in the room. Give competitors ninety seconds to eat the candy, and encourage teenagers to cheer for their representatives. When time is up, declare a winner, and have students shout, "You're number one!" and applaud. Ask:

- **How did you feel during this game?**
- **How are these feelings like confidence?**
- **How can we make friends feel like confident winners in real life?**
- **How do others build your confidence?**

Say: **True confidence is feeling good about yourself. It's an ability to face life's challenges knowing that God loves you. God is the source of our confidence.**

Opener Option 2: Full of Confidence

You'll need paper plates, scissors, and the box of celebration accessories you prepared before the meeting.

Give each student a paper plate. Say: **We're going to fill our plates with symbols of confidence. But first describe confidence for me—liking yourself or knowing God loves you and made you special, for example.**

Display the box of celebration stuff, and set out the scissors. Challenge teenagers each to fill their plates with symbols of confidence—an inflated balloon, sprinkles of confetti, or a construction paper happy-face, for example.

When students have finished, discuss the confidence symbols. Then have students form two teams, and place teams at opposite sides of the room. Challenge teams to walk their confidence-filled plates across the room. Explain that each person must protect his or her confidence while trying to remove the other team's confidence. Add that students may not touch other people's plates but that they can use methods such as blowing. Afterward ask:

- **How did you remove others' confidence?**
- **How did you try to protect your plateful of confidence?**
- **How can someone take away your confidence in daily life?**
- **How can you protect your confidence?**
- **How do you grow more confidence?**

Say: **Confidence is like fuel. It gives us power to try to succeed. God is the ultimate source of our confidence. Although people sometimes take**

LEADER TIP

If you have a smaller group, adapt both opener options and the "Bible Experience" by letting teenagers compete or work individually.

away our confidence, God frequently works through others to give us a boost of confidence.

Bible Experience: Verses of Confidence

You'll need Bibles and the box of celebration accessories you prepared before the meeting.

Have students form groups of two or three, and give each group a Bible. Have volunteers read Philippians 4:4-13.

Set the box of (remaining) celebration stuff in the middle of the room. Say: **I'm going to assign each group a verse we just read. I'll whisper the verse so other groups don't hear. Your group's task is to use items from the box to "design" your verse. Other groups will try to guess what your design portrays. For example, for Philippians 4:4—"Rejoice in the Lord always. I will say it again: Rejoice!"—a group could outline a body shape with ribbon. Inside the heart area, group members could place a construction paper smile.**

Assign each group a verse, and give groups a few minutes to design their verses. When groups have finished, let students walk around and guess other groups' verses. Afterward ask:

- What do these verses tell us about confidence?
- How does God give us confidence to face life's struggles?
- How do people help to give us confidence to face struggles?

Reflection: Why I Matter

You'll need index cards, pencils, tape, and the newsprint formula you prepared before the meeting.

Say: **You can confidently succeed in the midst of life's challenges because God has made you "W.H.O." you are. Only you can do the things you do.**

Give each student an index card and a pencil. Tape up the sheet of newsprint with the "W.H.O." formula. Allow time for students to complete the three sentences on their cards. Then have students form pairs and share answers.

Choose Your Closing

Closing Option 1: Listen to the Music

You'll need a Bible, pencils, and index cards from the "Reflection: Why I Matter" activity.

Say: **Believers during Bible times often sang songs about the security and confidence God gave them.** Ask a volunteer to read aloud Isaiah 26:1-4 as an example. Ask:

- **What do these words of praise tell us about how God gives us confidence?**

Say: **Now you and your partner can create a song with these words: "I can do it, and you can, too." You can include other words, but these must be the theme words.** Have students write their songs on the back of their index cards from the previous activity.

After they've finished, ask volunteers to sing their songs. Lead students in applauding each song.

Closing Option 2: Caring Commitment

You'll need index cards and pencils.

Give each person an index card and a pencil, and have each person sign his or her name. Gather and shuffle the cards, and place them face down in the center of the room. Have students form two groups. Have groups take turns choosing a card and naming three things that person is good at—friendship, school, art, sports, relaxation, Bible study, or creativity, for example. Afterward ask:

- **How have you boosted others' confidence this past week?**
- **How can you help others by boosting their confidence in the coming week?**

Have students form pairs and commit to building each other's confidence during the coming week. For example, partners could write a positive note to each other or pray for each other.

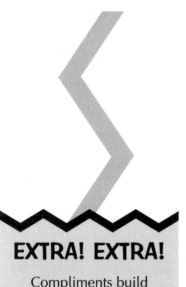

EXTRA! EXTRA!

Compliments build confidence. Most experts agree that it takes nine or ten positive comments to offset one negative comment. Build a "slam-free" environment—no negative comments allowed—by making this sign out of construction paper and hanging it in your youth room. On the sign, encourage your junior highers to write positive comments about each member of the group.

De-Stressing Stress

Why This Meeting Is Important

Junior highers face a world full of worries and stress—alcohol, zits, homework, tests, and the opposite sex—the list seems endless. Today's teenagers wonder how God's peace can replace their fears. Help your teenagers understand the influence God can have on the stress in their lives.

What Students Will Learn

In this meeting junior highers will
- understand how stress can hurt them,
- explore how God can bring peace, and
- use God's Word to reduce their stress.

Before the Meeting

Read the meeting, and gather supplies.

If you choose the "Have a Coke and Some Stress" opener, you'll need an unopened can of your group's favorite carbonated drink. Slide the tab to one side. Then with an ice pick, make two small holes in the can. Empty the can by holding it upside down and shaking it. Fill the can with water. Once it's full, seal the holes with a small drop of wax.

Supplies

You'll need Bibles, paper, pens, and a hat for each student.

Additional supplies for optional activities: a can of soda, an ice pick, water, drops of wax, wooden building blocks, newsprint, a marker, tape, a dictionary, index cards, a candle, and a matchbook.

Choose Your Opener

Opener Option 1: Have a Coke and Some Stress

You'll need the specially prepared can of soda.

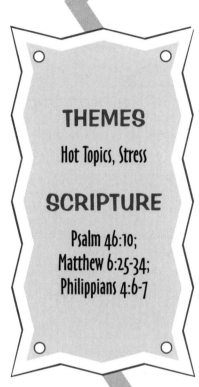

THEMES

Hot Topics, Stress

SCRIPTURE

Psalm 46:10;
Matthew 6:25-34;
Philippians 4:6-7

LEADER TIP

To fill the can, turn the water faucet on very low (this may take awhile), or make only one hole and use a syringe to fill the can.

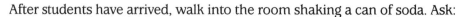

After students have arrived, walk into the room shaking a can of soda. Ask:

- **What's a good definition of stress or anxiety?**

Continue shaking the can. Ask:

- **What causes stress in your life?**
- **When you're stressed, how do you feel?**

Continue shaking the can while students answer your questions. When the conversation dies down, ask:

- **Who would like to open this can?**

Give students time to express their concerns or uneasiness about opening the can, and then ask:

- **How is this can like stress?**
- **Does your life ever feel like the contents of this can?**

Have a volunteer open the can. Give students a chance to express their feelings about the can not exploding with soda, and then say: **Today we're going to see how stress affects us in our daily lives.**

Opener Option 2: The Building Blocks of Stress

You'll need wooden building blocks, a marker, tape, and newsprint.

Tape a sheet of newsprint to a wall. Have teenagers come up with a list of things that stress them out, and write this list on the newsprint. Dump the blocks on the floor, and have students sit around the blocks. Say: **I'll read the things from the list. If the thing I read causes you stress, take a block or two and begin stacking them. If they fall over, you may rebuild your stack.** Read the items off the newsprint list slowly, giving students time to build their stacks. When you're finished reading the list, ask:

- **What does your stack tell you about stress?**
- **When have you felt like the tower of blocks? the fallen blocks?**

Say: **Today we're going to see how stress affects us in our daily lives.**

Bible Experience: Take a Chill Pill

You'll need Bibles, paper, and pens for each group.

Have teenagers get into pairs or trios. Distribute the Bibles, paper, and pens. Speaking quickly, say: **I'm going to read a Scripture, and I want your group to look it up and answer this question: " What does God say about dealing with stress and anxiety?" Make a long list.** Read aloud Matthew 6:25-34 as quickly as possible. Don't answer students' questions or repeat anything. Give students ninety seconds to answer the question. While they're answering, continually ask them to hurry up and remind them that time is almost up.

When time is up, slowly say: **Next I'm going to read Philippians 4:6-7. Please turn to that Scripture.** Give students plenty of time to find the Scripture. Then read the verses very calmly and peacefully. Afterward ask:

- What does God say about dealing with stress and anxiety? Give students ninety seconds to answer the question with another list.
- Which list is a better list?
- How did you feel trying to answer the question when you were rushed? when you weren't rushed?
- Which way seemed like the right way to read these verses?
- What are some ways that we can cope with stress in our lives?

Reflection: Hats

You'll need enough hats for each person to have one.

Pile all the hats in the center of the floor. Invite your junior highers to sit in a circle around the hats. Challenge them as a group to put the hats on each other. The catch is they can't use their hands or wrists to accomplish the task.

When everyone has a hat on, ask:

- How was this activity like or unlike the stress you face every day?
- What made this task difficult to accomplish?
- Why is it sometimes difficult to handle stress?
- What helped you to succeed?
- How can you successfully handle stress in your life?

Have students brainstorm stress-reducing ideas, and then say: **We can easily come up with things that are supposed to help us cope with stress, but none of these things will work unless we try them.** Ask:

- What's one thing you can do this week that'll help you reduce stress in your life?

Choose Your Closing

Closing Option 1: By Prayer and Supplication

You'll need a dictionary, pens, index cards, and one hat left in the center of the floor.

Give each person an index card and a pen. Say: **Write down some of the things you're stressed out about. You don't have to write your name on the card. When you're done, toss your card into the hat.**

After students have finished, read the definition of "supplication" from the dictionary. Say: **We're more than a group; we're a family. We can help each other deal with stress in a better way just as we helped each other put on those hats.** Have teenagers each pick one card from the hat, making sure they don't pick their own cards. Have students pair up and spread around the room. Say: **Talk with your partner about the effects of stress in your life. Then take turns praying for the person on your card.**

LEADER TIP

You may want to practice reading the verses in Matthew as quickly as possible. The faster you can read, the more stress teenagers will feel.

LEADER TIP

Some junior highers have a hard time being silent. If they're disruptive, ask them to leave. Have a volunteer go with them. Let them know they're not in trouble. They can make a snack or clean up the meeting room.

Closing Option 2: Be Still

You'll need a Bible, a candle, and a matchbook.

Take your group to the quietest, darkest room in the building. Once there, have your group spread out and sit comfortably. Light a candle, and place it in the middle of the room. Say: **I'm going to turn out the lights, and I want you to be as quiet as possible. You can close your eyes or look at the candle, but try not to look at each other. This is a serious time. Sometimes when life gets hectic, it's good to just stop and remember who's really in charge.**

Give the group a few minutes to settle down, and then read aloud Psalm 46:10. Let a minute pass, and then read the verse again, only slightly quieter. Repeat this several times, pausing for a minute between reading, until you're whispering. Then say: **You may leave at any time. Please try to leave as quietly as possible, and when you're out of the room, stay quiet out of respect for those remaining.**

Friendship

Why This Meeting Is Important

Few things are more important to adolescents than their friendships. Friends are a powerful influence—for good or bad. Use this meeting to guide junior highers in making and being the kind of friends who help, not hurt.

What Students Will Learn

In this meeting junior highers will
- identify qualities that make a good friend,
- evaluate their current friendships, and
- reflect on their own friendship qualities.

Before the Meeting

Read the meeting, and gather supplies.

Supplies

You'll need Bibles, self-stick notes, and pens.

Choose Your Opener

Opener Option 1: Quick Cliques

Say: **When I call out a description, find two other people who share that thing in common with you. For example, if I call out, "Same month of birth," try to find two people born in the same month as you. Each group must have exactly three members.**

Play several rounds of the game, calling out things such as "same eye color," "go to the same school," and "same middle initial." Afterward ask:
- **How is this activity like how groups are formed at your school?**
- **Why did some people get left out when the groups formed?**
- **Do people sometimes get left out of groups at school?**

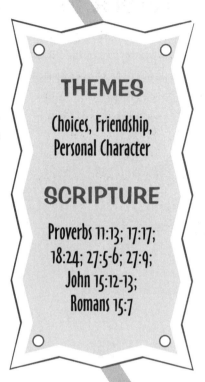

THEMES

Choices, Friendship, Personal Character

SCRIPTURE

Proverbs 11:13; 17:17; 18:24; 27:5-6; 27:9; John 15:12-13; Romans 15:7

LEADER TIP

If your group is too big or your meeting space is too small to have all the pairs compete at once, do the wheelbarrow race as a relay.

LEADER TIP

You may want to write the Scripture references on a sheet of newsprint so groups can discuss them at their own pace.

Say: **There's nothing wrong with hanging around people you have things in common with. But there's more to making good friendships than that. Let's take a look.**

Opener Option 2: Wheelbarrow Race

Hold an old-fashioned wheelbarrow race. Have kids form pairs. Have one partner hold the other's feet and race to one end of the room, trade roles, and then race back. After the race ask:

- What's the hardest thing about a wheelbarrow race?
- Which did you like better: holding your partner's feet or having your partner hold your feet? Why?
- How is friendship like a wheelbarrow race?

Say: **Just as we couldn't do a wheelbarrow race without a partner, most of us couldn't get along very well without friends. But like this race, sometimes our friendships can be a little awkward! Let's look at what God has to say about successful friendships.**

Bible Experience: What Makes a Good Friend?

You'll need Bibles, self-stick notes, and pens.

Have teenagers form groups of four. Give each group Bibles, self-stick notes, and pens. In their foursomes, have students look up and discuss the following passages: Proverbs 11:13; 17:17; 18:24; 27:5-6; 27:9; John 15:12-13; Romans 15:7. For each passage have groups discuss this question:

- According to this passage, what's one thing that makes someone a good friend?

Have someone from each group write the group's responses on separate self-stick notes. Groups will use the self-stick notes in the following activity. Also have groups discuss the following questions as they read each Scripture:

- Proverbs 11:13—Has a friend ever told your secrets to someone else? How did that affect your friendship?
- Proverbs 17:17—When do you especially need the support of a friend?
- Proverbs 18:24—What kinds of friends "ruin" you? How does a real friend show loyalty?
- Proverbs 27:5-6—How might being corrected feel like a slap in the face? How could correction help you? Do you think it takes a stronger friend to tell someone something they're doing wrong or to remain silent about it? Explain.
- Proverbs 27:9—Which of your friends can you count on to give you good advice?

- John 15:12-13—What are some of the sacrifices you might have to make for your friends? How can Jesus' love for you help you make those sacrifices?
- Romans 15:7—Without naming names, what are some things you find it hard to accept in other people? How can being more accepting help your friendships? How can it "bring praise to God"?

Reflection: Model Friends

You'll need the self-stick notes that groups wrote on in the previous activity.

Say: **Your job is to create a model friend. Choose one member of your foursome to be the "demonstration model"; the rest of you will be the salespeople. Attach your self-stick notes to the demonstration model where you think they fit—for example, a note about keeping secrets could go near the model's mouth.**

Have the foursomes take turns presenting their demonstration models. Ask each of the three salespeople in each group:

- **Which feature—things listed on the notes—of this model do you think is most important?**

When each group has had a turn, have students take off the self-stick notes but save them for later. Then ask:

- **What would your friendships be like if you and your friends had all the qualities we've discussed?**
- **Do you have some friendships that are hurtful to you instead of helpful?**
- **What do you think you should do about those friendships?**
- **Can you think of some people you'd like to make friends with who do have these qualities?**
- **How could you get to know those people better?**

Encourage your teenagers to be smart enough and brave enough to move out of damaging friendships and to build healthy friendships. Then have teenagers pray in their foursomes for specific things they need to do in their friendships.

Choose Your Closing

Closing Option 1: You're a Good Friend

You'll need the self-stick notes that groups wrote on earlier.

Say: **In your foursomes, spread out the self-stick notes and look at those qualities again. Choose one person to be your new demonstration model. Each of the rest of you will choose a quality of friendship you've**

LEADER TIP

In a mixed-gender group, have a guy play the role of the demonstration model to avoid any embarrassment in placing the self-stick notes.

seen that person demonstrate, hand him or her the note that describes that quality, and say how you've seen that person demonstrate that kind of friendship. Go around the group until each member of your foursome has been a demonstration model. It's OK to use the same self-stick notes more than once for different people.

Closing Option 2: What a Friend We Have in Jesus

You'll need the self-stick notes that groups wrote on earlier.

Have teenagers look again at the qualities they wrote on the self-stick notes. Say: **We aren't perfect friends, and most of our friends aren't perfect, either. But Jesus is. Choose a note that lists a quality of love or friendship that Jesus has shown to you; then come form one big circle.**

After teenagers have formed a circle, say: **We'll close with a circle prayer. When it's your turn, praise and thank Jesus for the way he shows the quality you chose, and ask him to help you become more like him in your friendships.**

Hope for the Hopeless

Why This Meeting Is Important

School pressures, physical changes, and relationship stresses can plunge junior highers into hopelessness. And when they look beyond themselves into a world filled with trouble, that sense of hopelessness can grow still more intense. Teenagers need a sure source of hope to cope with a complicated and often dangerous world. Use this meeting to point teenagers to God as their unfailing source of hope.

What Students Will Learn

In this meeting junior highers will
- identify situations in which they need hope,
- recognize God as the source of hope, and
- discover ways to tap into the hope God offers.

Before the Meeting

Read the meeting, and gather supplies.

If you choose the "Hope Chest" opener, prepare boxes each containing the following items: a Bible, a blanket, a food item, a rolled bandage, and a bottle of water. If you choose the "Cashing in Your Chips" opener, write the following situations (or make up your own) on separate sheets of paper: "Parents getting divorced"; "Moving to a new school"; "Failing school"; "No friends"; "Too tall/short/ugly."

Supplies

You'll need Bibles, pretzels, a bottle of a clear soft drink, paper cups, and markers.

Additional supplies for optional activities: boxes, blankets, food items, rolled bandages, bottles of water, ten poker chips for each person, masking tape, paper, pencils, and same-translation Bibles.

THEMES

God, Hope

SCRIPTURE

Psalms 42–43

Choose Your Opener

Opener Option 1: Hope Chest

For each team you'll need a box you prepared before the meeting.

Have students form teams of five. Line up teams at one end of the room, and place the boxes of items at the other end.

Say: **I'll assign each of you a situation. When I say "go," the first person on each team will run to the hope chest—the box—and find an object that can meet the need implied by your situation. Then that person will run back with the object and tag the next person in line.**

Go to each person on a team and assign one of the following situations: a homeless person on a cold night, a hungry child, a wounded person in a war-torn country, a person in a drought-stricken country, and a Christian in a country that persecutes Christians. Assign the same mix of situations to each team, but in a different order. Say "go!" to begin the relay.

After the relay, have students show their objects and explain how the objects would bring hope to their assigned situation. Ask:

- **What other ways can we help people around the world who feel hopeless?**
- **What needs can't be met with physical objects like those in our relay?**
- **When have you felt hopeless?**

Say: **It's easy to come up with reasons for people to feel hopeless in today's world. But even in the most difficult situations, there is hope.**

Opener Option 2: Cashing in Your Chips

You'll need ten poker chips for each person, masking tape, and the signs you prepared before the meeting.

Tape up the signs you prepared earlier around the room. Give each person ten poker chips. Say: **Imagine that these poker chips can be exchanged for hope to counteract the hopeless situations on the signs. Put chips by each sign according to how much buying power you'd need to overcome that situation—one chip for a minor problem, perhaps five or six for an extremely hopeless situation.**

When everyone's done, count the chips at each sign. Ask:

- **What makes the top "chip-getter" so hopeless?**
- **What other hopeless situations do you face?**

Say: **Hopelessness is a common feeling in today's world. But there is one source of hope we can all look to even in the toughest of situations. We'll explore that source of hope today.**

Bible Experience: Poetic License

You'll need Bibles, pretzels, and a bottle of a clear soft drink.

Distribute pretzels, and tell students to eat them. Meanwhile, have students form groups of no more than four and tell each other about times they've felt hopeless. After a few minutes, hold up the soft drink, but explain that no one can have a drink yet. Set the soft drink out of reach of your group but still in plain sight. Ask:

- Now that you've had some salty food, how does this soft drink look to you?
- What's it like to feel really thirsty?
- How is the way you feel as you look at the soft drink like the way people feel when facing a hopeless situation?

Read aloud Psalm 42:1-2a. Ask:

- What does it mean to be "thirsty" for God?
- How did you feel as you listened to this description?

Say: **King David knew what it was like to face seemingly hopeless situations. He wrote a two-part poem about hope and hopelessness when he was being hunted down by King Saul. In the poem he used vivid comparisons to express how he felt.**

Have students form four groups. Give each group a Bible, and have students turn to Psalms 42 and 43. Assign each group one of the comparison verses in Psalm 42 (verses 1, 3, 7, and 10). Give students eight minutes to gather any supplies from outside or inside your meeting place to demonstrate what's described in their verses. For example, the group demonstrating verse 3 might go to the kitchen, pour salt and water into cups for the rest of the group to drink, and then talk about what it would be like to have only tears for food.

After each group demonstrates its verse, ask:

- What emotions does this description bring up in you?
- When have you felt those emotions before?

Reflection: Thirst Quencher

You'll need Bibles, the clear soft drink, paper cups, and markers.

Give each person a paper cup filled with the soft drink to drink. Have students keep their cups. Read aloud Psalm 42:1 again. Ask:

- How does it feel to have something to drink now?
- How can God be like a thirst quencher?
- How was God the solution to David's problems?
- How can God be the solution in our hopeless situations?

Have students form trios, and distribute markers and Bibles. Say: **Read** through Psalms 42 and 43 in your trio. Every time you find a solution to hopelessness—such as "Put your hope in God" in Psalm 42:5—write it on your cup.

Have one person from each trio tell about the solutions they found. After each solution, ask for ways teenagers could apply that solution in their own lives. Have teenagers keep their cups to remind them that God is their source of hope.

Choose Your Closing

Closing Option 1: Psalms for Today

You'll need same-translation Bibles, paper, pencils, and masking tape.

Give each person a Bible, pencil, and sheet of paper. Say: **Write a line or two for a contemporary poem about hopelessness. You might write a poetic description of what hopelessness feels like, or you could describe a seemingly hopeless situation.**

Collect the papers, and then have teenagers turn to Psalm 42:11. One at a time, read aloud teenagers' poems. After each one, have the whole group read aloud Psalm 42:11 in unison. Then tape the poems teenagers wrote to a wall.

Close by having teenagers form pairs and pray for their partners to seek God as the source of hope when things seem hopeless.

Closing Option 2: Antiphonal Reading

You'll need same-translation Bibles.

Give each person a Bible. Say: **David knew that God was the answer to his feelings of hopelessness. We, too, can seek God when situations seem hopeless. As we close with a Bible reading, focus on the message in the verses you'll read in unison. And remember to turn to these verses when things aren't going well in your life.**

As your closing prayer, read aloud Psalms 42 and 43. Have students join in by reading the "chorus" sections—Psalms 42:5-6a, 11; 43:5—in unison.

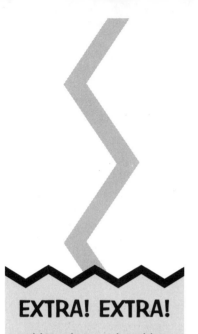

EXTRA! EXTRA!

Although David and his band of men were the "good guys," they shared much in common with today's gangs: a sense of alienation, the threat of violence, and the possibility that they would die young.

If gang involvement is an issue with your teenagers, encourage them to look at David's life and explore how he dealt with pressure and potentially negative situations. Have students retell 1 Samuel 23:7–24:22 in a contemporary setting and explore David's options.

Peer Pressure

Why This Meeting Is Important

A Teenage magazine survey revealed that 80 percent of teenagers give in to peer pressure at least once a week. Teenagers hate it when others pressure them, and yet 60 percent pressure others. Fewer than half are willing to do anything to stop peer pressure.

This meeting will help junior highers examine the effects of negative peer pressure and discover ways they can be a positive pressure in the lives of others.

What Students Will Learn

In this meeting junior highers will
- identify areas in which they feel pressured,
- learn what the Bible says about judging and influencing others, and
- discover and apply the benefits of positive peer pressure.

Before the Meeting

Read the meeting, and gather supplies.

If you choose the "Shake It Up" opener, cover a section of the floor with plastic trash bags, and use duct tape to secure the edges. Also write the following sources of peer pressure on separate index cards (write all five sources on an index card for yourself):
- "Having the perfect body"
- "Keeping up with current styles"
- "Knowing the right people"
- "Using drugs and alcohol"
- "Being sexually active"

Tape each card to a can of soft drink. You'll need one index card and can for each student. You'll also need a can of soft drink for yourself.

THEMES

Choices, Friendship, Hot Topics, Peer Pressure, Personal Character, Sin

SCRIPTURE

Genesis 3:1-24;
Psalm 40:10-17;
Proverbs 27:17;
1 Corinthians 10:13

Supplies

You'll need Bibles, small balloons, sharpened and unsharpened pencils, masking tape, and a pencil sharpener.

Additional supplies for optional activities: plastic trash bags, duct tape, index cards, canned soft drinks, a pen, paper, an empty wastebasket, a marker, and newsprint.

Choose Your Opener

Opener Option 1: Shake It Up

You'll need the trash bags you taped down and the cans of soft drinks with index cards you prepared before the meeting.

Distribute the soft drinks. Have students gather in groups according to the pressures on their soft drink cans. Say: **As you enjoy the soft drinks, talk about the pressures on your index cards. When have you experienced them? When have you caused others to experience them?**

After teenagers finish their discussions, stand on the trash bags and hold up your soft drink can. Shake your can as you read each item on your card. Say: **These are only a few of the pressure situations you might find yourselves in. We've all felt pressured to do or be what others want us to do or be. And when that pressure gets too great** (carefully open the can), **the results can be disastrous.** Ask:

• How was this explosion like or unlike the effects of peer pressure?

Say: **Today we'll discover some surprising ways we can ease peer pressure in each other's lives.**

Opener Option 2: Pressure Cooker

You'll need paper, pencils, and an empty wastebasket.

Distribute pencils and paper. Have teenagers write on their papers their biggest sources of peer pressure. Then have teenagers wad up the papers and toss them in the wastebasket.

Shake the papers around in the wastebasket as you say: **This is our peer pressure cooker. All of these sources of peer pressure are stewing around in here. Unfortunately, our peer pressure cooker has lost its lid, so it just might explode!**

Toss the papers out of the wastebasket. Have teenagers pick up the papers and then gather in groups of three to discuss their experiences with the pressures on the papers they've picked up.

After a few minutes of discussion, ask:

• How was our peer pressure cooker explosion like or unlike the effects of peer pressure?

Say: Sometimes peer pressure can create explosive situations with our friends. Other times its effects are much more subtle. Today we'll examine the ways peer pressure impacts our relationships.

Bible Experience: You Be the Judge

You'll need Bibles and a small balloon for each person.

Have students stand. Give everyone a balloon. Say: **We can't help but notice when others pressure us. But we may not be aware of the ways we pressure others. If you've ever pressured others in the ways I describe, blow two breaths into your balloon. If your balloon pops, sit down.**

Read the following items until everyone is seated. You may need to increase the number of breaths for each item or add additional items that fit your group. Say:

- **If you've ever asked, "Where'd you get that shirt?"**
- **If you've ever asked, "Have you seen [name of current movie]?"**
- **If you've ever asked, "Have you heard [name of popular band]'s new CD?"**
- **If you've ever discussed your love life with your friends.**
- **If you've ever chosen to do something with one friend over another.**
- **If you've ever tried to talk anyone into or out of something.**

After everyone is seated, say: **Look around you—you're in good company. We all influence and are influenced by our friends. Most of the time, we don't even think about it.**

Have students turn to partners and discuss these questions:

- **In what areas do your friends most influence you?**
- **Does it matter if the friends are Christian or non-Christian? Explain.**
- **In what areas do you most influence your Christian friends? your non-Christian friends?**

Say: **Let's take a look at how some biblical characters influenced others.** Have teenagers get into groups of three or four. Have groups read Genesis 3:1-24 and discuss the following questions:

- **Who influenced whom in this Scripture passage?**
- **What was the serpent's motivation in influencing Eve? Eve's motivation in influencing Adam?**
- **How would this story have ended differently had the pressure been positive instead of negative?**
- **What are your motivations when you pressure others?**

When groups have finished discussing, have them share their insights with the whole group.

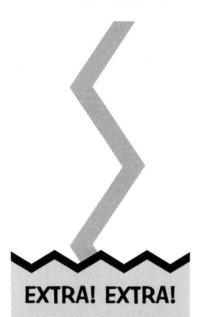

Reflection: Sharper Partners

You'll need sharpened and unsharpened pencils, masking tape, and a pencil sharpener.

Have teenagers form pairs, and give each person a sharpened pencil and an unsharpened pencil. Say: **Proverbs 27:17 says, "As iron sharpens iron, so one man sharpens another." Wouldn't it be great to have friends who "pressured" you to do your best, to be yourself, and to act out your faith?**

Think about an area in which you'd like to improve. Write a word that represents that area on a piece of masking tape, then wrap the tape around your unsharpened pencil. Pause. **Now tell your partner about your area. Take a few minutes to talk and pray about ways you can "sharpen" each other.**

After a few minutes of discussion, have students sharpen each other's pencils as reminders to sharpen each other this week.

Choose Your Closing

Closing Option 1: Prayer for Courage

You'll need a Bible, paper, and pencils.

Read aloud Psalm 40:10-17. Say: **It can take a lot of courage to be yourself when you're pressured to blend in. Take a few minutes to write your own prayer for courage.** Invite volunteers to share their prayers. Encourage teenagers to post their prayers in their lockers.

Closing Option 2: Escape Hatch

You'll need a Bible, a marker, masking tape, and newsprint.

Read aloud 1 Corinthians 10:13. Have teenagers brainstorm ways out of the temptations that peer pressure brings their way. Post teenagers' responses on a sheet of newsprint.

Close by encouraging teenagers to keep these "escape routes" in mind as they face peer pressure this week.

EXTRA! EXTRA!

Teenagers will have an easier time coping with negative peer pressure if they have a firm grasp on their own beliefs. Give each person an index card. On the top of the cards, have teenagers write, "Who I Am and Who I Am Not." Then have students write statements that define who they are and actions that follow from those statements. For example, someone might write, "I am kind and considerate. I do not make fun of others." Encourage teenagers to keep their cards at school to remind them of their beliefs.

Prescription for Life: No Drugs

Why This Meeting Is Important

Drug abuse is one of the greatest menaces our young people face. Most teenagers will, at some point, have the opportunity to resist the temptation to use drugs. Use this meeting to help your students make the right choice about drugs.

What Students Will Learn

In this meeting junior highers will
- experience the effects of involvement with drugs,
- respond to pressure to be involved with drugs, and
- explore the consequences of drug use.

Before the Meeting

Read the meeting, and gather supplies.

Supplies

You'll need Bibles, photocopies of the "Fast Facts" handout (p. 79), pencils, and paper.

Additional supplies for optional activities: three large gumballs of different colors, newsprint, markers, and star stickers.

Choose Your Opener

Opener Option 1: Gumball Gambit

You'll need three large gumballs of different colors.

Have students form a circle, and ask a volunteer to stand in the middle. Show students the gumballs, and tell them the volunteer will try to catch people who are holding or have held a gumball. Explain that teenagers can each pass the gumballs to anyone but that the gumballs have to be in

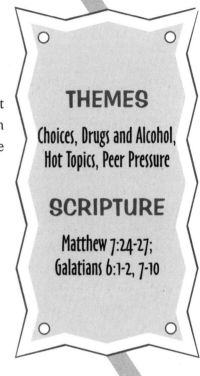

THEMES

Choices, Drugs and Alcohol, Hot Topics, Peer Pressure

SCRIPTURE

Matthew 7:24-27; Galatians 6:1-2, 7-10

someone's hand at all times. While the volunteer closes his or her eyes and spins around five times, hand the gumballs to three people.

Have the volunteer open his or her eyes. Explain that the volunteer should point at someone to accuse that person of holding a gumball. If the person is holding a gumball, he or she must confess and step out of the circle. Then the volunteer can check the hands of two other people in the circle. If people have traces of the same gumball color as the "guilty" person, they're "guilty by association" and must also step out of the circle. If either of these two people is holding a gumball, the volunteer may check the hands of two more people. Then have the volunteer close his or her eyes, spin around five times, and begin again.

After several minutes or when the volunteer has found all the gumballs, ask:

- How did you feel as you held the gumballs?
- How did you feel when someone was caught who could make you guilty by association?
- How did you feel if you were caught? if you weren't?
- How is this gumball like drugs in real life?
- How is this game like being around drugs?

Say: It's impossible to be around drugs without being affected. Whether you actually use drugs or associate with people who do, your life can become stained by drugs.

Opener Option 2: Concerns

You'll need newsprint and markers.

Have teenagers form groups of four to six. Give a sheet of newsprint and a marker to each group. Ask groups to think about things they see happening in their families, schools, neighborhoods, and communities as results of drug and alcohol abuse.

After a few minutes of brainstorming, ask groups to discuss these questions:

- In what ways are teenagers affected when they use alcohol or drugs?
- In what ways are others affected when people use alcohol or drugs?

Have groups take turns reporting what they discussed to the whole group.

Bible Experience: Fast Facts

You'll need Bibles, photocopies of the "Fast Facts" handout (p. 79), and pencils.

Distribute pencils and the "Fast Facts" handouts. Designate one side of the room as "true" and the opposite side of the room as "false." As you read aloud each question, have teenagers move to answer true or false.

After each question, read and discuss the answer. Encourage students to jot down notes on their handouts. Afterward ask:

- **What is difficult about making decisions concerning alcohol and other drugs?**
- **How can you decipher what's true and false about the effects of drugs?**

Have students form two groups. Have one group read Galatians 6:1-2, 7-10 and the other group read Matthew 7:24-27. Then ask groups to discuss this question:

- **Based on these verses, how do you think you should respond to pressure to use drugs?**

Ask each group to prepare a one- or two-sentence statement based on the Scripture that the group read to help teenagers respond biblically to the pressure to use drugs. Have groups share their statements with each other, and encourage teenagers to write the statements on the back of their handouts.

ANSWERS TO "FAST FACTS" HANDOUT

1. False. All kinds of teenagers drink.
2. True.
3. False. Often young people begin experimenting with drugs around fifth or sixth grade.
4. False. Alcohol is.
5. False. Tobacco smoke contains many drugs including nicotine and tar.
6. True.
7. False. Chemicals from marijuana stay in the body for a month or more.
8. False. Many teenagers, by their own admission, drink for the sole purpose of getting drunk.
9. False. Teenagers are trying all kinds of drugs, and use of drugs such as crystal methamphetamine, heroin, and cocaine is rising.
10. True.

Reflection: Passing Notes

You'll need paper and pencils.

Distribute paper and pencils to students who need them. Explain that you'd like students to pretend they've been handed three notes from friends. Tell students that you'll read aloud the contents of the notes and that they should write a response to each note.

Say: **The first note says, "I need your help. I'm afraid the principal's going to search my locker today, and I need you to hide my weed in** your locker." Pause for students to write a response. Then say: **The second note says, "Hey, we have a chance to be invited to *the* party of the year this weekend! All we have to do is bring some beer. I can count you in, right?"** Pause for students to write a response. Then say: **The third note says, "I just wanted to give you a 'heads up.' I told my mom I'm coming to your house tonight. Really, though, I'm going to Brian's house to smoke some ice."** Have teenagers form pairs and share their responses with each other. Then have pairs discuss these questions:

- Do you think people your age face situations like these? Why or why not?
- From the Bible passages we read earlier, how do you think God would want you to respond in these situations?
- How can you use what you've learned today to address pressure you face or will face to use drugs?

Choose Your Closing

Closing Option 1: Friendship Images

Ask teenagers to get comfortable, perhaps by lying on the floor or relaxing in chairs, and close their eyes. Tell teenagers you're going to have them imagine situations involving someone they care for. As you say the following, pause between statements so teenagers can think and imagine. Say: **Think of someone you know who's involved with drugs. This could be a friend, a family member, a neighbor, or even yourself. If you don't know anyone, think of someone you would be concerned about in this situation.** Pause. **What is this person doing? What does he or she look like? How are drugs or alcohol affecting this person in areas of family, school, friends, and physical health? What do you see in this person's future? How do you feel toward this person? How do you feel about what he or she is doing? What would you like to say to this person?** Pause. **Now pray for the person you're thinking about.** Pause. **Finish your prayer by asking God to help you when you're faced with choices about drugs and alcohol.**

Closing Option 2: Star Affirmations

You'll need star stickers.

Say: **In Philippians 2:15, the Apostle Paul says we can "shine like stars in the universe."** Distribute a star sticker to each person. Have students find a partner and tell that partner how he or she has been a "shining star" to others. Then have partners exchange star stickers.

Close the meeting with a short prayer of thanks for all the shining stars in your group.

Fast Facts

TRUE OR FALSE?

1. Good students and teenagers involved in sports or church activities are less likely to drink.

2. For young people who drink, the average age to start drinking is around twelve.

3. Most young people don't try drugs until they're in high school.

4. Cocaine is the most widely abused drug in the United States.

5. Cigarettes contain no drugs.

6. Often young people are "turned on" to drugs by older brothers and sisters.

7. The 450 known chemicals in marijuana stay in the body for several days.

8. There is no difference between teenagers drinking and adults drinking socially.

9. Drugs aren't really a problem with teenagers because most of them are experimenting with alcohol.

10. People who have a strong self-esteem, feel good about themselves, and have strong support tend to resist pressure to use drugs and alcohol.

Permission to photocopy this handout from *High-Energy Meetings for Young Teenagers* granted for local church use.
Copyright © Group Publishing, Inc., P.O. Box 481, Loveland, CO 80539.

THEMES

Conflict, Family, Hot Topics

SCRIPTURE

Matthew 5:14-16; 11:28-30; Romans 8:31-32, 38-39; 12:17-21; 1 Corinthians 10:13; Ephesians 3:16-18; Hebrews 13:5b

LEADER TIP

This meeting is especially designed for a group of eight or fewer. You can use it as a by-invitation-only meeting for teenagers with divorced parents, as a special-interest session during a retreat, or with your entire group. If you use it with your entire group, have teenagers form smaller groups for each activity. You may also ask adult volunteers with whom the group feels comfortable to lead each smaller group through the meeting.

Why This Meeting Is Important

Every junior higher faces family problems, whether it's sibling rivalry or alcoholism or divorce. Use this meeting to reach out to your teenagers, to engender group members' support for one another, and to encourage them with God's Word.

What Students Will Learn

In this meeting junior highers will

- identify feelings about their home situations,
- look in God's Word for support, and
- set goals to do their part for harmony at home.

Before the Meeting

Read the meeting, and gather supplies. Cut out a large cross from newsprint.

Supplies

You'll need Bibles, scissors, newsprint, markers, paper, and pencils. Additional supplies for optional activities: a bag.

Choose Your Opener

Opener Option 1: Knots

Have everyone stand in a circle, and say: **Put your hands in the center of the circle. Grab and hold two different people's hands, and make sure they're the hands of people not standing next to you.** Pause for students to react. **Now, without letting go of any hands, untangle yourselves.**

If group members quickly accomplish this task, have them repeat the process. Afterward ask:

- How was this activity like family problems we experience sometimes?
- What's difficult about untangling family problems?

Say: **We all get tangled up in family problems sometimes, and we need time and cooperation to work things out. We'll discover some support today to help us through that process.**

Opener Option 2: Newsprint Symbols

You'll need newsprint.

Give each person a sheet of newsprint. Have teenagers each tear out or shape their newsprint into a symbol that represents how they feel about their family. For example, someone might tear the newsprint into strips to show that family members are torn apart, or someone might crush the newsprint into a ball to demonstrate anger.

After students have created their symbols, ask them to form trios and explain their symbols to their trio members. Ask:

- How easy or difficult would it be to make this newsprint look like it originally looked?
- How is that like how easy or difficult it is to solve family problems?

Say: **Family problems take a lot of time to develop, and they take a lot of time to heal. We'll discover some support today to help us through that process.**

Bible Experience: Scripture Support

You'll need Bibles, markers, and the newsprint cross you made before the meeting.

Distribute Bibles, and assign each person one of these Bible passages: Matthew 5:14-16; 11:28-30; Romans 8:31-32, 38-39; 12:17-21; 1 Corinthians 10:13; Ephesians 3:16-18; Hebrews 13:5b. Give students time to find and read their passages. Then have teenagers form a circle. Then, one by one, have students read their passages aloud and complete the following sentence: "The good news here for me is…"

As teenagers finish sharing, have them write on the newsprint cross how Jesus gives them hope about their family problems. Keep the cross in the center of the group. Ask:

- How does it make you feel to know that everyone faces family problems sometimes?
- How do these Scriptures affect how you'll approach family problems?
- How can these verses support you when you're dealing with family problems?

LEADER TIP

As junior highers open up about their homes during this meeting, listen with care and offer support. Don't judge, criticize, or act shocked. Your teenagers may be reluctant to talk about their feelings because they feel guilty, embarrassed, hurt, frightened, or angry. Encourage them to discuss, but don't force them.

LEADER TIP

Some junior highers will express frustration at this activity since so many family problems are out of their control. Assure students that you understand that they're not responsible for many of their families' problems. Then encourage teenagers to evaluate what they *realistically* can do to bring harmony to the family.

If you hear students making commitments such as "I'll get rid of all my anger" or "I'll make my parents' relationship new by helping them remember why they loved each other," gently discuss how they think they can accomplish those goals and how they think they can change broad feelings— especially others' feelings. Help redirect students toward specific, realistic behaviors that they can control.

Reflection: Personal Goals

You'll need paper, pencils, and the newsprint cross.

Distribute paper and pencils to the group. Have students create two columns on their papers. Tell students to label one column, "One thing I want to get rid of" and the other column, "One thing I want to make new." Then have students fill in their columns with commitments to deal with family problems. Encourage students to think of specific behaviors that may help the family. Say: **For example, someone could write, "I want to get rid of my habit of picking on my sister" and "I want to make new my commitment to help with dinner." Tailor your commitments to your own family's situation.**

After everyone has finished, have teenagers form pairs and share what they wrote. After they've shared what they want to get rid of, have them tear that column from their papers and throw it away to symbolize being rid of it. After students have shared what they want to make new, have them fold the paper, write their names on the outside, and place it near the newsprint cross. Then have pairs discuss the following questions:

- **How can your partner help you follow through on your commitments?**
- **How can God help you follow through?**
- **What's one thing you can do this week to address each commitment you made?**

Choose Your Closing

Closing Option 1: Dear Abby

You'll need paper, pencils, and a bag.

Distribute two sheets of paper and a pencil to each person. Say: **We're going to support each other in a fun, anonymous way. We're going to write questions about our family problems, and then we'll answer each other's questions.**

Have each student write one question about a problem on each sheet of paper, and remind students not to put their names on their papers. When students have finished, have them put their questions in a bag.

Pass the bag around, and have each person take a turn drawing a question and reading it aloud. After each question, have group members respond with ideas.

Afterward, close the meeting with a prayer, asking God to help teenagers with their problems. Have students take home their commitment papers from the Reflection activity as reminders of their desire to make things new.

Closing Option 2: Thanksgiving

Invite everyone to stand in a circle and join hands. Encourage teenagers to offer a prayer of thanks for their families. Close the prayer by asking God to help group members support each other through difficult family times. Afterward close with a group hug. Have students take home their commitment papers from the Reflection activity as reminders to make things new.

LEADER TIP

If a student writes a question that indicates abuse is taking place, be sure to encourage that student to talk to you, a pastor, or another trusted adult right away. Be aware that some states require you to alert public authorities if you discover that a student is being abused, and be sure to help that student find professional help.

Sex Respect

THEMES

Choices, Hot Topics, Love, Opposite-Sex Relationships, Peer Pressure, Sin

SCRIPTURE

Psalm 46:7;
Matthew 6:31-33;
John 16:33;
1 Corinthians 2:9; 6:18-20;
1 Thessalonians 4:3-8

Why This Meeting Is Important

In the United States, the average age for first having sex is fifteen for girls and fourteen for guys. Help your junior highers understand the true value of sex and the negative consequences of sexual experience outside of marriage.

What Students Will Learn

In this meeting junior highers will
- analyze the consequences of bad sexual choices,
- evaluate their own sex respect, and
- commit to increasing their sex respect.

Before the Meeting

Read the meeting, and gather supplies. Write the word "sex" on pieces of masking tape, and stick the tape to tubes of super glue. Also write the word "forgiveness" on pieces of masking tape, and stick the tape to different tubes of super glue. Prepare a newsprint poster titled, "The Great Sex Debate." On the poster, write the following:

"If you have sex outside of marriage, you're likely to
- break up with your partner before you marry him or her,
- turn away anyone who wants to marry a virgin,
- be less happy in your marriage,
- get a divorce,
- commit adultery after you marry,
- marry for the wrong reasons,
- eventually be less satisfied with your married sex life,
- spoil sex due to conditioned feelings of guilt and remorse
(from Ray Short's *Sex, Love, or Infatuation*).
Scripture passages of comfort as you face the future:
- Psalm 46:7
- Matthew 6:31-33

- John 16:33
- 1 Corinthians 2:9"

Supplies

You'll need Bibles; markers; masking tape; tubes of super glue; blue, pink, and red construction paper; and newsprint.

Additional supplies for optional activities: the "dating" section of a newspaper, photocopies of the "Then-What Tree" handout (p. 88), pencils, and paper.

Choose Your Opener

Opener Option 1: Love Wanted

You'll need the "dating" section of a newspaper.

Have students form groups of four. Distribute ads from the dating section. Have teenagers read through some ads and then discuss the following questions:

- **What does it seem like these people are really looking for—love or sex? What's the difference?**
- **What kind of respect for sex do these people appear to have?**

Afterward say: **Today we're going to talk about sex respect—respect for the power of sex and for God's protective guidelines. We demonstrate our sex respect by how we conduct ourselves physically in relationships with others.**

Opener Option 2: The Then-What Tree

You'll need photocopies of the "Then-What Tree" handout (p. 88) and pencils.

As teenagers arrive, distribute photocopies of the "Then-What Tree" handout and pencils. Have students work alone to fill in the rectangles by following different branches of the tree, starting at the bottom. Encourage teenagers to try different branches and fill in all the rectangles.

After a few minutes, have everyone form a circle and share their answers. Compare the consequences of different choices. Discuss how sometimes saying no seems worse at the time but ends up being a better choice. Ask:

- **Which of these branches demonstrates a respect for sex?**

Say: **Today we're going to talk about sex respect. Sex respect is respect for the power of sex and for God's protective guidelines. We demonstrate sex respect by how we conduct ourselves physically in relationships with others.**

LEADER TIP

It's a good idea to let parents know when you'll be doing this study. Encourage parents to call you with questions before the meeting and then to talk about sex with their teenagers after the meeting.

LEADER TIP

Be aware that some of your students already may have had sexual experiences and will be uncomfortable with this topic. Be sure to communicate hope and not condemnation. Your goal is to educate, restore, and heal rather than scold or punish.

Bible Experience: Never the Same

You'll need a Bible; the tubes of super glue you prepared before the meeting; blue, pink, and red construction paper; a marker; masking tape; and newsprint.

Give each teenager two sheets of construction paper—one blue and one pink. Explain that you're going to tell a story and that students will use the paper to demonstrate what happens. Say: **After Blue and Pinky had been dating for almost a year, they went to a school dance together and danced all evening. After the dance was over, they went for a ride together. Blue drove to a secluded place. Blue and Pinky started kissing, and one thing led to another until they had sex.**

Distribute the tubes of glue labeled "sex." Have students each glue their pink and blue sheets of construction paper together. Then ask:

- **How did you feel as I told this story?**
- **How would you change the story if you could?**

Ask teenagers to separate their glued sheets of construction paper. One sheet of paper will have the color of the other sheet of paper on it. Ask:

- **What's different about Blue or Pinky now?**
- **How do the sheets of paper show the effects of premarital sex?**

Read aloud 1 Corinthians 6:18-20, and tape up a sheet of newsprint. Ask:

- **How are sexual sins against your own body?**
- **What are some physical consequences of having sex outside of marriage? spiritual consequences?**

List on the sheet of newsprint the consequences students name. Ask teenagers to identify long-term consequences—consequences that will last for life. Say: **This Scripture says you were bought at a price. You are very valuable to God. Imagine again that Blue and Pinky are real people.**

Give each person two sheets of red construction paper. Distribute the tubes of glue labeled "forgiveness." Have each student glue a sheet of red construction paper to Blue and then to Pinky.

Say: **The good news is that Jesus can forgive the sin of sex outside of marriage. Jesus can cover the sin with the price he paid for you— his blood. You can be forgiven, but you will still have to face the consequences of sin.**

Reflection: The Great Sex Debate

You'll need Bibles, markers, masking tape, and the newsprint poster you prepared before the meeting.

Have teenagers form groups of four to six. Tape up the newsprint poster you prepared before the meeting. Have group members discuss how premarital sex could affect their future families. Distribute Bibles, and have groups read the Scriptures listed on the newsprint. Then have each group write on the poster a one- or two-sentence statement that comforts them as they think about their future.

Choose Your Closing

Closing Option 1: 1-555-FOR-LOVE

You'll need Bibles, paper, and pencils.

Have teenagers form groups of three. Distribute Bibles, paper, and pencils. Tell groups they're going to run a phone service, but this phone line is going to give a positive message. Have groups each read 1 Thessalonians 4:3-8 and write a message they'd use to promote God's standards of sex within marriage and sex respect. Encourage teenagers to include clear instructions of God's standards, a warning about the consequences of premarital sex, and a message of God's forgiveness to those who might've already broken God's commandments.

Have groups share their messages with each other. Then close in prayer, asking God to help kids maintain a healthy respect for sex.

Closing Option 2: Commitments

You'll need paper and pencils.

Have students sit alone, and distribute paper and pencils. Ask students to think about a commitment they'd like to make concerning sex. For example, students may want to commit to waiting for sex until they're married. Have students write or draw a symbol of their commitments on their papers, and assure them that no one will see their papers. Ask students to sign their commitments.

To close, lead teenagers in a prayer like this one: **Dear God, thank you for teaching us how to have respect for sex. Please help me with this commitment I've made today.** Pause for students to silently finish the prayer.

THE THEN-WHAT TREE

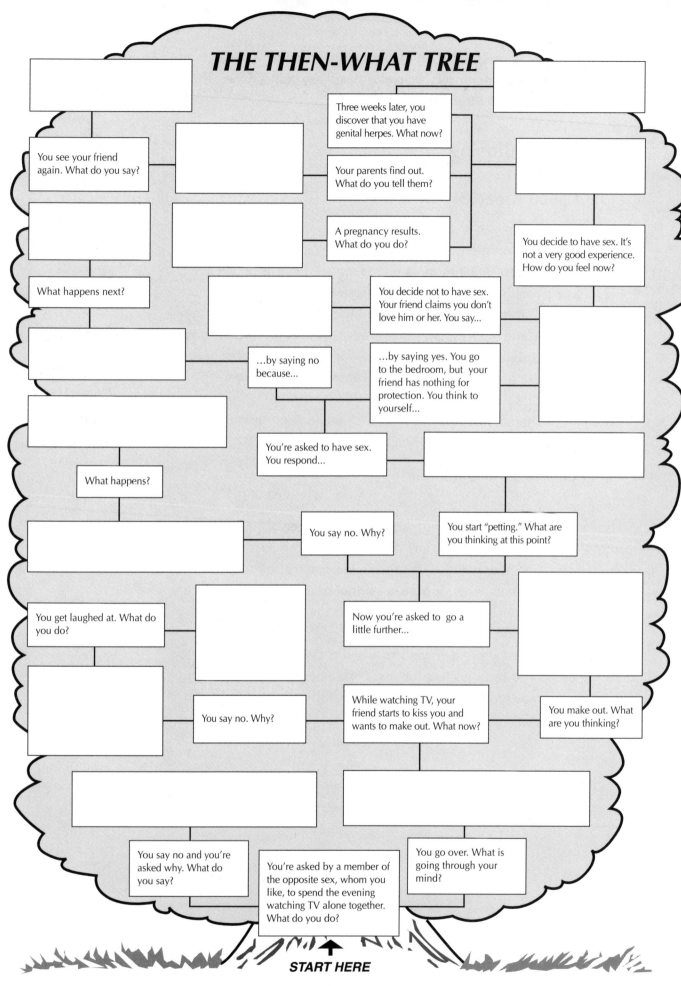

Three weeks later, you discover that you have genital herpes. What now?

You see your friend again. What do you say?

Your parents find out. What do you tell them?

A pregnancy results. What do you do?

You decide to have sex. It's not a very good experience. How do you feel now?

What happens next?

You decide not to have sex. Your friend claims you don't love him or her. You say...

...by saying no because...

...by saying yes. You go to the bedroom, but your friend has nothing for protection. You think to yourself...

You're asked to have sex. You respond...

What happens?

You say no. Why?

You start "petting." What are you thinking at this point?

You get laughed at. What do you do?

Now you're asked to go a little further...

You say no. Why?

While watching TV, your friend starts to kiss you and wants to make out. What now?

You make out. What are you thinking?

You say no and you're asked why. What do you say?

You're asked by a member of the opposite sex, whom you like, to spend the evening watching TV alone together. What do you do?

You go over. What is going through your mind?

START HERE

Permission to photocopy this handout from *High-Energy Meetings for Young Teenagers* granted for local church use.
Copyright © Group Publishing, Inc., P.O. Box 481, Loveland, CO 80539.

What's Love About?

Why This Meeting Is Important

To most teenagers the word "love" means "romance." They don't connect love with what our attitude should be toward all people—even those kids they might dislike at school. This meeting seeks to show that love is a conscious decision to place value on other people. Christian love means valuing others because Christ values all of us.

What Students Will Learn

In this meeting junior highers will

- explore the value they place on other people,
- grapple with the idea that God finds value in everyone, and
- find ways to love people they might not like.

Before the Meeting

Read the meeting, and gather supplies. Tape off six three-foot square areas on the floor, arranged in a circle, with about fifteen feet between each area if possible. Also, create a list of six to ten pairs of activities teenagers might enjoy doing. You'll ask teenagers to choose which activity in each pair they prefer, so use pairs of activities such as "skateboarding or in-line skating," "shopping or eating out," and "playing basketball or mountain biking."

Supplies

You'll need Bibles; masking tape; twenty-five or thirty objects that move differently when slid or rolled, such as Ping-Pong balls or batteries (you can have more than one of each item); paper; and a pen.

Additional supplies for optional activities: pencils and index cards.

THEMES

Friendship, Love

SCRIPTURE

Isaiah 53:5-6;
Matthew 18:10-14;
Luke 15:1-10;
1 John 3:10-11, 14-20;
4:7-21

Choose Your Opener

Opener Option 1: The Love Boat

You'll need paper and pencils.

Give everyone a pencil and a sheet of paper, and then say: **Let's pretend you're going on a cruise. You're allowed two hundred pounds of gear other than necessities, and whatever you carry has to be whatever you want to spend the most time with. Go!**

After about two minutes, have students form groups of no more than eight. Have group members share what they listed and why. Then ask:

- **What was the most or least surprising thing you saw someone take? Why?**
- **By what criteria did you make your choices?**
- **In real life what makes one thing more or less valuable than another thing?**

Say: **When we say we love something, that usually means we've made a decision to value it. During this meeting we're going to talk about love, especially as it applies to the value we place on other people.**

Opener Option 2: Choosing Sides

Select a couple of volunteers, and then say: **Let's begin this meeting with a little game. This game involves some pretty intense physical activity, but before we begin let's choose sides.** Have the volunteers choose participants from the group. When the volunteers have chosen, say: **After looking at these teams and our space, I'm not sure we should play the first game. Let's pick some new teams and play a trivia game instead.**

Select two new volunteers, and go through the process of choosing sides again. When volunteers have chosen, say: **OK, this won't work either. Let's stick to something creative like working on a craft. I promise you: This is the last time we'll choose sides.**

Have new volunteers choose teams, and then stop and say: **In case you haven't already guessed, the game we were really playing was choosing sides. I wanted to see how you would choose people for the different teams.** Ask:

- **How did you decide who would be on each team?**
- **How did you feel about who chose you and when?**
- **How did you feel about doing the choosing?**
- **How is this like life in the real world?**

Say: **Our meeting today is about the way we choose people to be our friends and who we choose to love. With that in mind, let's look a little more deeply at what love means.**

Bible Experience: Hard Mentality

You'll need Bibles, the taped-off areas, and the objects that move differently when slid or rolled.

Hold up one of each of the objects, and have students name each object after a different group at school—nerds, jocks, and skaters, for example. Then have students form three teams, and assign each team to one of the six taped-off areas. Place an equal mixture of items within each team's area.

Say: **The object of this game is for your team to get as many of your objects as you can into your "home" territory on the opposite side of the circle from you. You'll have one minute to do this. But you can touch the objects with your feet only, and you're all to do this at the same time. Keep in mind who the objects represent as you move them across the space. Let your feelings about these different groups of kids affect the manner in which you move the objects and if you'd want them in your home territory.**

When all the teams are ready, start the game. After a minute call time, and have teams see which objects made it into each team's area. Ask:

- **What made this game easy or difficult?**
- **What types of people did you want or not want in your territory? Why?**

Have a person from each team read one of the following passages aloud to the rest of the group: Isaiah 53:5-6; Matthew 18:10-14; Luke 15:1-10. Ask:

- **How do you understand these verses in light of what we just did?**
- **How was your team's action like or unlike the Scriptures you read?**
- **Why don't we treat people as we'd want to be treated?**
- **When have you been loved and accepted? shunned?**

Reflection: Common Ground

You'll need the list of pairs of activities teenagers might enjoy doing that you created before the meeting.

Say: **I'm going to read a list of activities, and I want you to gather to one side of the room with other people who prefer the same activity as you. For example, if I say, "in-line skating or skateboarding," those of you who prefer in-line skating should move to one side of the room and those who prefer skateboarding should move to the other side of the room. For each pair I read, you have to choose one activity or the other.**

After students understand the instructions, read between six and ten preferences. Then gather the group back together, and ask:

- **What did you learn about others by doing this?**
- **What did you learn about yourself?**

- Do you have some surprising things in common with others? Explain.
- Do you think you might have something in common with the groups of people you labeled in our previous activity?
- What keeps us from getting to know others more deeply?

Choose Your Closing

Closing Option 1: Cheer Value

You'll need index cards and pencils.

Have students form a circle, and give everyone an index card and a pencil. Have each person write his or her name in the upper left-hand corner of the card, and say: **As we conclude our discussion of love, I want to remind you again that all of us are loved by God and are therefore worthy of love from God's people. For the next few minutes, I'd like you to pass the cards around the circle and write something about each person that makes him or her unique and special. When your card comes back to you, hold onto it.**

Have teenagers pass the cards around the circle, making sure that your card is included in the mix. Then have kids each pass their cards to the person to the right. Say: **Now I want our group to end this session with a cheer for each person here. For the cheer, the reader says, "[Name on the card] is special because [he or she] is [comments on the card]." Then all of us will shout together, "And we love you, [the person's name]!"**

Have students take turns reading. Afterward close with a prayer, asking God to help the group members find ways to express God's love to others. As students leave, give them back their cards with the comments written on them.

Closing Option 2: Make-Up Exam

You'll need Bibles, paper, and pencils.

Give each person a Bible, pencil, and sheet of paper. Have volunteers read aloud 1 John 3:10-11, 14-20; 4:7-21. Then say: **God's standards for authentic Christian behavior are clear in these words. Our love for God is measured by the extent to which we are willing to love others. As a reminder of this, and also of how difficult this is to put into practice, I'd like you to give yourselves an exam. List as many as five ways you think you might not have measured up to this high standard over the past week. When you're through, say a silent prayer, asking God to help you in each area in the coming week.**

LEADER TIP

This can be a difficult exercise for younger junior highers. Try to affirm every response or lack of response. It's also helpful if everyone in your meeting room, including volunteers and leaders, participates fully.

Section 3

CELEBRATING HOLIDAYS

New Year's Meeting: Happy New You!

THEMES

Choices, Priorities, Spiritual Growth

SCRIPTURE

John 3:1-8; 1 Peter 1:3-9

Why This Meeting Is Important

Junior highers are in the midst of change, and they *want* to change. The new year is a great time for them to take stock of where they are in life and where they want to be. Use this meeting to help your group members celebrate the new people they are in Christ, set meaningful and realistic goals for themselves, and decide how to reach those goals.

What Students Will Learn

In this meeting junior highers will

- consider where their current choices may take them,
- see God as a positive influence for change, and
- create goals for themselves.

Before the Meeting

Read the meeting, and gather supplies.

If you choose the "Celebration Countdown" opener, first estimate the number of students you'll have. Then, using four different colors of paper—blue, red, yellow, and green—cut out a slip of paper for each student. Make sure you have nearly equal numbers of each color. Then write the following incomplete sentences on the different slips of paper:

- "A positive step I took last year was…" (on blue slips)
- "I felt stepped-on last year when…" (on red slips)
- "To step closer to God, I need to…" (on yellow slips)
- "A step I wish I'd not taken is…" (on green slips)

Then insert each slip of paper into a balloon and blow up the balloon. Use a dark-colored marker to write a number on each balloon, from zero to the number of participants in the meeting.

Supplies

You'll need Bibles, a wastebasket, scrap paper, paper, pencils, and photocopies of the "Goal-Setting Guidelines" and "Goal Areas" handout (p. 99).

Additional supplies for optional activities: blue, red, yellow, and green paper; scissors; a pen; a dark-colored marker; and balloons.

Choose Your Opener

Opener Option 1: Two-Step Opener

Have junior highers line up near the middle of the room and face one end of the room. Say: **I'm going to read some statements about the path you've chosen for your life. If you agree with a statement, take two steps forward. If you disagree with a statement, take one step backward.** Read aloud the following statements:

- I achieved an important goal in the last year.
- I'm sure the steps I'm taking in my life right now won't lead to a dead end.
- I've never stepped on someone else to achieve a goal.
- I've felt God directing my steps.
- I've made long-term goals for my life.
- I've made short-term goals for my life.
- God's will is an important influence on the goals and decisions I make.
- The new year is an exciting opportunity for personal growth and change.
- I talk to my parents and friends about my hopes and fears for the future.
- I know the steps I need to take to accomplish my goals.

Afterward ask:

- How was this activity like trying to reach goals?
- Have you thought about how to reach specific goals? Why or why not?

Opener Option 2: Celebration Countdown

You'll need the numbered balloons you prepared before the meeting.

Give each person a balloon. Say: **The new year is upon us, and many of you are thinking about changes—or resolutions—you'd like to make in your life. First let's do a special countdown to the new year. Look at the number on your balloon. When I call out your number, stomp on your balloon and pop it. Then find the secret statement that's hidden in your balloon, and keep it.**

Together with the students, count down the numbers. Then say: **Each of you has a colored slip of paper from your balloon. There are four colors: blue, red, yellow, and green. Form a group of four that includes each color.**

In their groups, have students each read aloud their incomplete sentences and add how they'd complete the sentences. Then ask them to trade papers and each complete the new sentences. Have students continue to trade papers until each group member has completed all four sentences.

Bible Experience: New-Birth Olympics

You'll need Bibles, a wastebasket, scrap paper, paper, and pencils.

Have teenagers form teams of three, and have equal numbers of teams stand in each corner of the room. Give each person three pieces of scrap paper to wad into balls. Place a wastebasket in the center of the room.

Say: **This activity is called the New-Birth Olympics. There are nine separate "events" in this Olympics. The object is for your team to throw as many paper wads as possible into the wastebasket. Team members will take turns until you've completed all nine events.** Have teams all shoot at the same time for each event and keep track of how many shots they make. Here are the events:

1. Close your eyes and shoot.
2. Look to your right as you shoot.
3. Use your left hand if you're right-handed or your right hand if you're left-handed.
4. Shoot over your left shoulder.
5. Hold the paper wad in your mouth and shoot it.
6. Shoot between your legs.
7. Hold hands with someone and shoot holding the paper wad together.
8. Throw the paper wad in the air and bat it toward the basket.
9. Put the paper wad on your foot and shoot.

Afterward say: **The goal of these events was to shoot the paper wads into the basket. But that goal was difficult—sometimes impossible—to achieve because our chosen methods were ineffective.**

Have students sit with their teams. Give each team a Bible, a sheet of paper, and a pencil. Ask them to read John 3:1-8 and 1 Peter 1:3-9 and then discuss and write down their answers to the following questions:

• What does it mean to be "born again"?
• What must you do to be born again?
• What's the "proof" of your faith?

After a few minutes, ask a representative from each team to read aloud the team's answers. Then say: **In some ways starting a new year is like being born again. You're given a chance to start over. Let's see how much better we can reach our Olympic goals if our method is "born again."**

Give each team three paper wads. Have students stand close to the wastebasket, face it, and throw the paper wads into the basket.

Reflection: Goal-Setting

You'll need photocopies of the "Goal-Setting Guidelines" and "Goal Areas" handout (p. 99) and pencils.

Distribute pencils and photocopies of the "Goal-Setting Guidelines" and "Goal Areas" handout. Say: **We can talk and dream about things we'd like to change or accomplish, but setting practical goals for ourselves is the best way to reach our goals. A good goal should be simple, achievable, specific, and easy to evaluate. These goal-setting tips are listed on your handout. Some examples of goals that meet the guidelines are "I will read my Bible for five minutes every day for three months" and "I will introduce myself to three new people at the next retreat."**

Have students remain in groups of three. Say: **Write your name on your handout. Then write a goal for yourself in each of the areas listed in the "Goal Areas" box. When everyone in your group finishes, take turns sharing one goal and how you intend to accomplish it.** After everyone has finished, encourage teenagers to take home their goals and follow through.

Choose Your Closing

Closing Option 1: Where Am I Headed?

Designate the four corners of the room as "a," "b," "c," or "d." Say: **I'm going to read a number of statements that have four possible endings: a, b, c, or d. After I read each statement, stand in the corner that best represents your feelings.**

Read the following aloud, pausing for students to stand in corners. As you read each statement and teenagers choose a corner to stand in, ask a few teenagers why they chose their answers. Say:

1. In the coming year, my current friendships will

   (a) stay the same.

   (b) get weaker.

   (c) get stronger.

   (d) end.

2. In high school I think I'll

   (a) get a car.

   (b) drop out.

   (c) make new friends.

   (d) get good grades.

3. In the next year, I expect to

   (a) have a girlfriend or boyfriend.

   (b) become more independent.

(c) decide what I want to do with my life.

(d) have fun.

4. In five years I want my relationship with God to

(a) become much closer.

(b) be just the way it is now.

(c) be the focus of my life.

(d) be in the background of my life.

5. When it comes to my career choice, I

(a) know exactly what I want to do.

(b) have lots of options.

(c) don't need to think about it now.

(d) will let what happens, happen.

6. I involve God in my decisions and goal-setting by

(a) seeking help by praying and reading the Bible.

(b) talking to my Christian friends and adults I respect.

(c) evaluating my options by considering what a Christian would do.

(d) leaving all my decisions to God.

Closing Option 2: Countdown Prayer

Have students form a circle. Explain that you'll start a prayer and that students will each pray silently for ten things as you count down to the new year. Start the prayer by saying: **Dear God, thank you for this new year. Please help us with these five things this year.** Pause. **We also want to thank and praise you for these five things.** Pause for students to finish the prayer.

Goal-Setting Guidelines

1. Make it simple.

2. Make it achievable.

3. Make it specific.

4. Make it easy to evaluate.

Goal Areas

1. Spiritual (relationship with God)

2. Relational (relationship with friends)

3. Personal (how I feel about myself)

4. Academic (how well I do in school)

Permission to photocopy this handout from *High-Energy Meetings for Young Teenagers* granted for local church use.
Copyright © Group Publishing, Inc., P.O. Box 481, Loveland, CO 80539.

Valentine's Day: Jesus, God's Valentine

THEMES

Jesus, Love

SCRIPTURE

John 3:16-17;
1 Corinthians 13:4-8

LEADER TIP

Saint Valentine's Day was established to honor a third-century martyr. We celebrate this holiday by sending cards to family, friends, and loved ones. Help teenagers see that God loved us so much, he sent us the greatest valentine—Jesus.

Why This Meeting Is Important

Did you ever make Valentine's Day mailboxes when you were younger? I remember decorating old shoe boxes and lining them up along the counter beneath the classroom window. As Valentine's Day came closer, our boxes expanded with loads of cards—or so we hoped. Every year some kids wouldn't get as many cards. And every year, those forgotten kids would be devastated. It's no wonder so many people have grown up thinking they'll never be loved. Use this meeting to help teenagers understand that God loves them—no matter who they are, what they look like, or how many abilities they possess.

What Students Will Learn

In this meeting junior highers will

- recognize the differences between how God and the world describe love,
- understand that God communicated his love for them by sending them Jesus, and
- give and receive God's love.

Before the Meeting

Read the meeting, and gather supplies. Cut out fifteen construction paper hearts. On each heart write one of the "love descriptions" listed in 1 Corinthians 13:4-8—for example, "Love is patient" and "Love is kind." Tape the hearts to a wall so the writing is hidden.

If you choose the "Love-Song Mania" opener, prepare to play a few seconds of different well-known love songs from CDs or recorded from the radio. You'll also need to cut a twelve-inch red heart from construction paper.

If you choose the "Heartthrob Mania" opener, collect a few posters or magazine photographs of celebrity heartthrobs. Tape small paper strips over identifying features such as eyes, smiles, or hair. Tape the posters or pictures to a wall.

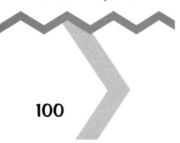

If you choose the "God's Valentine Box" closing, decorate an old shoe box with Valentine's Day stickers and hearts. Then cut a mail slot in the top.

Supplies

You'll need Bibles, scissors, red construction paper, a pen, masking tape, paper, and markers.

Additional supplies for optional activities: CDs and a CD player or tapes and a tape player, posters or magazine photographs of celebrities, a shoe box, Valentine's Day decorations such as stickers or hearts, glue, newsprint, pencils, and envelopes.

Choose Your Opener

Opener Option 1: Love-Song Mania

You'll need the twelve-inch construction paper heart, the CDs or tapes you prepared before the meeting, newsprint, masking tape, and a marker.

Have students form two teams. Have teams each line up on opposite sides of the room. Place the construction paper heart in the center of the room. Play the first few seconds of a well-known love song. The first person to run to the center, tag the heart, and correctly identify the song wins a point for his or her team. Award teams a bonus point if they can name the recording artist as well. Record the points on newsprint taped to a wall.

After the game, total the points and award the winning team a round of applause. Ask:

- **How do popular songs describe love?**
- **How do these descriptions compare to the way God might describe love?**

Say: **Popular music often describes love differently from the way God describes love. In this meeting we'll learn more about God's love.**

Opener Option 2: Heartthrob Mania

You'll need the celebrity posters or pictures you prepared before the meeting and masking tape.

As students enter the room, have them look at the posters or pictures and try to identify the heartthrobs. See who guessed correctly, and then reveal the heartthrob identities. Ask:

- **What qualities do these heartthrobs have that makes us love them so much?**
- **How does this type of love compare to the way God might define love?**

Say: **God's love is different from anything we've ever experienced. In this meeting we'll learn more about God's love.**

LEADER TIP

Instead of recording love songs or using CDs, ask students to list popular love-song titles on newsprint. Or record students singing some of their favorite love songs. Instead of collecting celebrity posters, ask students to share names of famous celebrity heartthrobs. List the names on newsprint. Ask the group to vote and rank them in order of popularity.

Bible Experience: Love Hits the Target

You'll need Bibles, the fifteen construction paper hearts you prepared before the meeting, masking tape, and a paper wad.

Invite junior highers to stand ten feet away from the wall where you have taped the fifteen construction paper hearts. Have students each throw the paper wad and try to hit a heart. As students each hit a heart, have them take it down and read the love description on the back. When they finish reading, have them retape the hearts to the wall so the writing shows.

After all of the hearts have been turned over, ask students to read 1 Corinthians 13:4-8. Ask:

- **How do these biblical love descriptions compare to the earthly descriptions from our opening?**

Say: God's love is better than anything we've seen or heard on television, the movies, or radio. Something this good needs to be shared with everybody.

Reflection: Getting the Good News Out

You'll need a Bible, red construction paper, and markers.

Have students form pairs or trios. Give each pair or trio a sheet of red construction paper and a marker. Say: **Your pair** [or trio] **represents God's Valentine Manufacturing Company. Your job is to create a valentine to communicate God's awesome love for his people.**

After a few minutes, ask kids to read their valentines—"Good news, Valentines! We'll live forever because God loves us so much," for example.

Have a volunteer read aloud John 3:16-17. Ask:

- **How do you feel knowing that God sent Jesus as a sign of his love?**
- **How can you share God's love with others?**

Choose Your Closing

Closing Option 1: Jesus Loves Me

You'll need the fifteen construction paper hearts.

Have volunteers read the love descriptions on the hearts, substituting "Jesus" for the word "love"—for example, "Jesus is patient" and "Jesus is kind." Then say: **When you feel down and not very lovable, remember what Jesus did for you and how much he loves you.**

Have volunteers read the heart descriptions again, this time inserting their own names after each phrase—for example, "Jesus is patient with Marissa" and "Jesus keeps no records of wrongs with Lucas."

Close in prayer, thanking God for his love.

LEADER TIP

Rather than a paper wad, use a toy bow-and-arrow set with rubber suction-cup tips on the arrows. Borrow a set from a church family with younger children, or buy an inexpensive set at a toy store.

Closing Option 2: God's Valentine Box

You'll need paper, pencils, envelopes, and the shoe box you prepared before the meeting.

Give each student a sheet of paper, a pencil, and an envelope. Have teenagers each write a valentine note to God, thanking him for his gift of love—Jesus. Have students sign their notes and place them in the envelopes.

Gather in a circle, and invite students to place their envelopes into God's valentine box. Ask your pastor to read aloud the valentines at your next worship service.

Close with a silent prayer, thanking God for his great gift of love—Jesus.

EXTRA! EXTRA!

Mail a valentine to each of your students the week after your meeting. Have the valentines be from Jesus, telling them he loves them!

Easter: Is There No Justice?

THEMES

Hope, Jesus, Justice, Sin

SCRIPTURE

Matthew 5:1-12; 12:14-21;
Luke 18:1-8; 23:32-46;
John 18:19-23, 28-40;
19:1-16;
Romans 3:25-26

Why This Meeting Is Important

Junior highers know about injustice firsthand. They know a fourteen-year-old who deserves everything but has nothing. They know that their parents are splitting up. They know kids who cheat and get away with it.

But these injustices are nothing compared to the Crucifixion. This lesson will help teenagers understand the incredible injustice done to Jesus and how he reacted to that injustice.

What Students Will Learn

In this meeting junior highers will

- experience injustice,
- explore the Crucifixion story, and
- discover how to live Christlike lives.

Before the Meeting

Read the meeting, and gather supplies.

Supplies

You'll need Bibles, paper, pencils, newsprint, and markers.

Additional supplies for optional activities: snack foods and drinks for half your group, supplies for a game of volleyball, and recent newspaper and magazine stories that represent injustices in the world.

Choose Your Opener

Opener Option 1: Unfair!

You'll need snack foods and drinks and supplies for a game of volleyball.

Open the meeting by setting out snack foods and drinks and then randomly choosing people who can enjoy the snacks. Be sure to leave out at least half your group members. Students can share if they so choose, but be sure to have a limited supply of snacks and drinks so students will have to think hard about giving up their goodies.

Then have students form two teams: one consisting of the people who had snacks, and one consisting of people who didn't. Set up a volleyball net, and have teams play a quick game of volleyball. Before starting, tell the team who had snacks that it must hit the ball exactly six times before hitting it over the net, and tell the other team it may hit the ball as few or as many times as desired. Play until one team gets ten points.

Then have students form groups of three to discuss the following questions:

- What was it like not to get a snack?
- How did you feel about playing the game with unfair rules?
- When have you experienced similar feelings in everyday life?

Say: We live in a world where things aren't always fair. Today we'll explore one of the most significant injustices in history and talk about how we can live out our faith even in the face of injustice.

Opener Option 2: No, This Is Worse!

You'll need recent newspaper and magazine articles about injustices in the world.

Have teenagers form teams of no more than four. Place the newspaper and magazine clippings around the room, and say: The object of this activity is to find the two stories with the worst examples of injustice and have them in your team's grasp when the time is up. Each team may pick up only two stories at a time and may trade with others in any way possible for stories they think are worse.

Begin the activity, and allow students to get a little wild as they try to find the worst stories. Call time after a minute or two. Then have teenagers describe the stories and award each an "injustice" value from one to five, with five being the most unjust. When you've determined point values for each story, collect the three highest, and give them to any team at random. Declare that team the winner. Then have teams discuss the following questions:

- How easy or difficult was it to determine the level of injustice in these stories?
- Why is there so much injustice in the world?
- How did you feel when I took the top stories and gave them to a different team?
- How is that like the way you feel when you've been unfairly treated?

Say: One of the most significant examples of injustice occurred almost two thousand years ago. We're going to explore that situation and how we as Christians should respond to injustice.

Bible Experience: The Biggest Injustice

You'll need Bibles, paper, and pencils.

Have teenagers form five groups. Give three groups Bibles, paper, and pencils. Give the other two groups one Bible to share. Say: **I'm going to assign a portion of Scripture to each group. Your job is to read the passage and look for ways that Jesus was treated unjustly or examples of how he reacted to that injustice. After a few minutes, I'll call time and ask groups to share their findings.**

Tell the groups without paper and pencils that they'll have to memorize their ideas since they can't write them down. If teenagers complain, explain that this is just another example of injustice that they'll have to live with.

Assign the following passages: John 18:19-23, 28-36, 37-40; 19:1-11, 12-16. Allow plenty of time for students to read and discuss their passages. Then have each group summarize its passage and insights for the whole group. Do this in the same order as the passages listed above. Then ask:

- How is the way Jesus was treated an example of injustice?
- How are the examples of injustice we see around us today similar to Jesus' story? How are they different?
- How was Jesus' injustice "worth it"?
- Have you ever suffered an injustice that was worth it?

Reflection: Our Response

You'll need Bibles, newsprint, and markers.

Have students form groups of no more than four. Assign one of the following passages to each group: Matthew 12:14-21; Luke 18:1-8; 23:32-46; Romans 3:25-26. After teenagers have read their passages, have them answer the following questions in their groups:

- What does this passage tell us about Jesus' response to injustice?
- What does it imply about how we should react toward injustice?
- What are right and wrong ways to respond to injustice?

When groups finish, have volunteers share their conclusions with the whole group. Ask:

- What's the cause of injustice?

Say: **Jesus hated injustice, yet when he was the target of injustice, he still forgave those who mistreated him. Jesus' sermon on the mount gives us good advice for how we might respond when we see someone hurt by injustice.**

Read aloud Matthew 5:1-12. Then have students list as many injustices as they can think of on a large sheet of newsprint. Encourage teenagers to think of things that may affect themselves or their classmates—or things that are more global in nature.

When the injustices have been listed, have teenagers brainstorm about how Jesus might have responded to each one. Then ask students to tell how they can respond to the injustices according to Jesus' teaching.

Say: **While we can't solve all the injustices in the world, we can pray for others and let them know that God is near and will ultimately bring justice to the whole world.**

Choose Your Closing

Closing Option 1: Righting the Wrong

Ask students to think of one injustice they can do something about and still behave in a Christlike way. For example, have students brainstorm ways to reach out in love to people they believe are acting unfairly at school. Have teenagers each choose a favorite idea, then encourage them to act on that idea. Close the meeting with a short prayer, thanking God for being just and asking for guidance when they face injustice in the world.

Closing Option 2: Prayer Meeting

You'll need the list of injustices created in the "Reflection: Our Response" activity.

Have students form groups of no more than four. Have each group choose an injustice from the list created earlier and spend two minutes praying for the people who are treated unfairly in that situation. Encourage students to pray for God's intervention and for their own wisdom to know how to respond to the situation.

Close by having students say a prayer of thanks to God for being a just God and for sending Jesus to take the full measure of our sinfulness in his death on the cross.

Thanksgiving: What Do You Take for Granted?

THEMES

God, Hope

SCRIPTURE

1 Samuel 21:10—22:1;
Psalm 56;
1 Thessalonians 5:16-18

Why This Meeting Is Important

"Thank you" doesn't cross our lips often enough. When circumstances get us down, we often feel that life "just isn't fair." We forget that God is worthy of thanks in *every* situation. Use this meeting to prepare your teenagers for Thanksgiving and to help them be thankful in all circumstances.

What Students Will Learn

In this meeting junior highers will
- discover that they take some things for granted,
- explore thankfulness in difficult situations, and
- brainstorm ways to be thankful.

Before the Meeting

Read the meeting, and gather supplies.

Supplies

You'll need Bibles, newsprint, tape, a marker, paper, and pencils.
Additional supplies for optional activities: paper cups, water, blindfolds, a watch with a second hand, thank you notes, and markers.

Choose Your Opener

Opener Option 1: Take It for Granted Relay

You'll need paper cups, water, tape, and blindfolds.
Have teenagers form groups of four. Have foursomes assign each person in the group one of the following roles: legs, hands, eyes, and arms. Have the legs sit against one wall of the room, the hands stand in the middle of the room, and the eyes and arms sit against the wall opposite the legs. Make sure that members of each group are lined up with one another.

Have the eyes put on blindfolds. Have the hands fold their thumbs against their palms, and then tape their thumbs to their palms. Hand each legs person a paper cup full of water. If there is an uneven number of teenagers, have the extra teenagers be hands, and have the hands help each other carry the water.

Say: **We're going to run a quick relay race. The legs will travel to the hands and give them the cups of water. The hands will bring the water to the eyes. The eyes will then serve the water to the arms. But the legs can't walk or crawl; they must scoot themselves along the floor without walking. The hands don't have use of their thumbs. The eyes are blind-folded, and the arms must drink the water while they hold their arms behind their backs.**

When students understand the game, say: **Ready? Go!**

After the race ask:

• **What's your reaction to this relay?**

• **Is there anything you take for granted in life? If so, what?**

Say: **Today we're going to talk about what we take for granted and how we have so much to be thankful for.**

Opener Option 2: Circle of Thanks

You'll need a stopwatch or a watch with a second hand.

When everyone has arrived, have students form a circle. Say: **Let's see how many things we can complain about in three minutes. I'll start, and we'll go around the circle to the right. When it's your turn, mention something to complain about. But there's one rule: You can't repeat anything anyone else has said. We have three minutes to go around the circle as many times as we can.**

When students understand the game, begin.

After three minutes play the game again. This time have students say things they're thankful for. Challenge them to go around the circle more times than they did with the complaints. Remind them that they can't repeat anyone else's answer. When the students are ready, begin.

After this second round, ask:

• **Which round of this game was easier: the first or the second? Why?**

• **Do you sometimes find it difficult to be thankful? Why or why not?**

Say: **Today we're going to talk about taking things for granted and being thankful in all circumstances.**

Bible Experience: Thanks in Crazy Times

You'll need Bibles, newsprint, tape, and a marker.

Tape a blank sheet of newsprint to a wall. Say: **Let's create a list of situations in which it's difficult to be thankful. If you have an idea, I'll**

LEADER TIP

If you have a physically challenged person in your group, give this person the edge by allowing him or her to choose a role first.

write it on the newsprint. But you can't tell me what your idea is. You must communicate it without speaking. You can act out, sign, or otherwise creatively communicate your answers to me. Write kids' ideas on the newsprint. Then ask:

- Was communicating in different ways difficult? Why or why not?
- What can you be thankful for in the creative ways you communicated?
- What makes it difficult to be thankful in the situations we listed?

Say: King David, a person in Bible times, faced difficult circumstances often. Let's read about one difficult situation in his life and how he responded to it. We'll read about a time when David was being pursued by Saul, the king at that time who was jealous of David. David spent quite a bit of his early adult life running from Saul, who wanted to kill him.

Have students form pairs and read 1 Samuel 21:10–22:1. Then have pairs discuss these questions:

- How was David's difficult situation like your difficult situation in communicating your ideas for our list? How was it different?
- What made this situation difficult for David?
- If you were in David's shoes, what would your attitude have been?
- How would you have felt toward God?

Then say: We have a record of how David responded to God in this situation. He wrote a psalm—a praise to God—that corresponds to this time in his life.

Have pairs read Psalm 56 and then discuss these questions:

- According to this psalm, how did David respond to God in his trying situation?
- How do you respond to God in difficult situations?
- Do you ever respond in the way David did? Why or why not?
- What are some things you can feel thankful for in the difficult situations we listed?

When pairs have finished their discussions, invite students to share their answers to the last question with the rest of the group.

Reflection: Thanks in All Things

You'll need Bibles, paper, and pencils.

Hand each person a Bible, a sheet of paper, and a pencil. Then encourage teenagers to find a place away from each other. Say: As you spend time reflecting, think of a personal situation in which it's difficult to feel thankful. For example, maybe you have a new stepparent you don't get along with. Write your situation on your sheet of paper. Then read

1 Thessalonians 5:16-18. After you've read the passage, think of one way it applies to your difficult situation and write it on your paper.

Allow students about five minutes to read and reflect. Then have teenagers return to their pairs and share with their partners what they wrote. Encourage teenagers to pray, thanking God that they can "give thanks in all circumstances," and to thank God for their partners.

Choose Your Closing

Closing Option 1: Thank You Notes

You'll need thank you notes and markers.

Say: **David's psalm to God was like a thank you note. Right now, write a thank you note to God, either about a tough situation you're experiencing or for something you usually take for granted. You can write a psalm like David did, or you can write a thank you note like you'd write to a friend or relative.**

When teenagers are finished, encourage them to take their thank you notes home and place them somewhere prominent, such as on a night stand, to remind them to be thankful at all times.

Closing Option 2: Giving Thanks at Thanksgiving

You'll need newsprint, tape, and a marker.

Tape a sheet of newsprint to a wall, and draw a vertical line down the middle of the newsprint. Have students brainstorm all of the things they eat on Thanksgiving. Write each item in the left column of the newsprint. Then have students brainstorm for each item a category of things to thank God for. Write the categories in the right-hand column of the newsprint. For example, for "turkey," the corresponding category could be "animals"; for "cranberry sauce," the corresponding category could be "things that are red." Encourage students to be creative!

After the group has brainstormed about all the categories, encourage students to use the items on their Thanksgiving tables this year to cue them to thank God for things. For example, when they see turkey, they could thank God for a pet they love, and when they see cranberry sauce, they could be thankful for their red Nike hightops.

LEADER TIP

If you don't have any thank you notes, bring paper and markers in various colors and have teenagers create their own thank you notes. If you have rubber stamps and ink pads, include them for teenagers to use.

Christmas: Turning Nobodies Into Somebodies

THEMES

Hope, Purpose, Self-Image

SCRIPTURE

Matthew 1:18-25;
Luke 1:26-45; 2:8-20

Why This Meeting Is Important

We can recycle almost anything. But God has been in the recycling business for thousands of years. He takes our empty lives and transforms them into lives full of purpose and meaning. Use this meeting to help teenagers discover how God recycles nobodies and turns them into somebodies.

What Students Will Learn

In this meeting junior highers will

- discuss recycling old things into new things,
- discover the Christmas-story Bible characters in a new light, and
- understand how God's love recycles them into spectacular somebodies.

Before the Meeting

Read the meeting, and gather supplies.

Supplies

You'll need Bibles, paper, scissors, pencils, and a clean plastic jug. Additional supplies for optional activities: pennies and apples.

Choose Your Opener

Opener Option 1: Extraordinary!

Welcome students, then have students form groups of no more than four. Tell them to search the room, find one ordinary item, and brainstorm an "extraordinary" use for it. When groups present their ordinary-turned-extraordinary item, they should say, "You may think this is a _____, but it's really a _____." For example, someone may say, "You may think this is a wastebasket, but it's really a large offering basket for all the world hunger money we'll collect Sunday" or "You may think this is a rug, but it's really a heavy-duty washrag for those tough-to-get-out stains."

Gather groups, and have them present their extraordinary items. Ask:

- How did you feel trying to think of extraordinary uses for ordinary items?
- What was easy or hard about it?
- How does God take our ordinary lives and make us extraordinary?

Say: **God takes our old, sinful lives and makes us new with his forgiveness. He turns nobodies into somebodies. Let's look at the Christmas story and see how God used ordinary people for this extraordinary plan of salvation.**

Opener Option 2: Recycle Brigade

Lead students outside around your church property. Ask students to pick up anything that can be recycled, such as pop cans, empty plastic bottles, newspapers, empty glass jars, and so on.

Gather students back inside, and have them place their items on a table. Ask:

- What do all these items have in common?
- What are some things that each of these can be recycled into?
- How are we like these items?
- How does God "recycle" us?

Say: **No matter what condition we're in, God changes us into something new. We begin as nobodies, and he turns us into somebodies. Today we're going to look at the Christmas story and see how God used ordinary people for an extraordinary plan.**

Bible Experience: Extraordinary Christmas Scenes

You'll need three Bibles.

Have students form three groups. Give each group a Bible and one of these passages: Matthew 1:18-25; Luke 1:26-45; 2:8-20.

Say: **In your group read your passage and discuss the moment God chose ordinary people for extraordinary purposes. Use everyone in your group to represent that moment. For example, for Luke 2:8-20, you could be shepherds kneeling on the ground looking up at angels. We'll take turns presenting our Christmas scenes. When it's your turn, arrange your Christmas scene, then freeze! Don't move. We'll try to guess the moment.**

After five minutes have each group freeze in its Christmas scene, and have others guess the extraordinary moment. Ask:

- Why do you think God chose ordinary people to carry out his extraordinary plan?
- What extraordinary ways can God use you to show others his love?

LEADER TIP

Set up a recycle station in your church. Find separate boxes for glass, aluminum, paper, and Styrofoam. Place the items students found in this activity in the boxes.

Reflection: Make It Useful

You'll need paper, scissors, pencils, and a clean plastic jug.

Give each person a slip of paper and a pencil. Say: **Think of at least one area in your life that makes you feel like a nobody—an area you'd like God to recycle into something new. For example, you might want help recycling your temper into patience. Write your area on your slip of paper, and then fold it.** Have students form groups of three, and have students tell about the area they've written.

Place an empty plastic jug in the center of the room. Say: **Pray for your group members and the areas they'd like to be recycled. When you're done praying, come to the plastic jug and put your paper inside of it.**

Choose Your Closing

Closing Option 1: What's It Worth to You?

You'll need a penny for each person.

Give each person a penny. Ask:

- **In what ways are pennies used over and over again?**
- **How are we like pennies?**

Say: **Pennies are used in stores, banks, restaurants, and allowances—in different ways and places—and their external appearance doesn't change. God works with us the same way. When God recycles us, we may look the same on the outside, but there's no telling how God will use us to show others his love.**

Have trio members tell each other one way they see God working in them—for example, "Johanna, when others see you smile and hear you laugh, they know it's fun to be a Christian." After group members affirm each other, have them swap pennies.

Encourage teenagers to keep their pennies as a reminder of God's work within them.

Closing Option 2: Planting Seeds

For each person, you'll need an apple.

Toss an apple to each person. Have teenagers eat until they see a seed. Ask:

- **What had to happen before a seed eventually produced the apple you're eating?**
- **How is a seed that grows into an apple like God making us into extraordinary somebodies?**

Say: **Just like apple seeds eventually grow to be trees that produce these apples, God takes our ordinary lives, plants his Word in us, waters**

EXTRA! EXTRA!

Label the jug "Recycled Worries," and leave it in your meeting room. Any time teenagers have prayer concerns, encourage them to write the concerns on separate slips of paper and drop them in the jug. As they think of the jug being recycled, have them think also of God's recycling, transforming work in their lives.

us with his love, and gives us the warm sunshine of caring people who guide us. God uses us for extraordinary purposes.

Close by offering a prayer of thanks for God's extraordinary work in teenagers' lives. Have them finish eating their apples and wish them a merry Christmas!

EXTRA! EXTRA!

Newspapers are filled with stories of ordinary people doing extraordinary things, such as teenagers serving homeless families. Challenge your teenagers to search the papers for stories of God using ordinary people for extraordinary purposes.

Christmas: Giving As God Gives

THEMES

God, Jesus, Service

SCRIPTURE

John 3:16-17;
Romans 6:20-23;
Ephesians 2:8-9;
Hebrews 9:24-28

Why This Meeting Is Important

In a society that places so much emphasis on *getting*, it can be hard for junior highers (like the rest of us) to remember the true meaning of Christmas. Use this meeting to help teenagers see that Christmas is not only a time for remembering the gifts God has given to humanity, but also for responding to those gifts by giving to others.

What Students Will Learn

In this meeting junior highers will

- talk about the true meaning of Christmas,
- compare tangible gifts with eternal gifts,
- discover gifts God has given us, and
- think of ways to respond to God's gifts by giving to others.

Before the Meeting

Read the meeting, and gather supplies. Write the following Scripture references on four small, separate pieces of paper: John 3:16-17; Romans 6:20-23; Ephesians 2:8-9; Hebrews 9:24-28. Place each piece of paper in a small box along with several pieces of candy, then gift-wrap each box. Also write the following questions on a sheet of newsprint:

- "According to these verses, what is one gift God has given us?"
- "What does this gift have to do with Christmas?"
- "What does this teach you about the true meaning of Christmas?"

If you choose the "Great Gift Ideas" closing, gift-wrap a large box.

Supplies

You'll need Bibles, small boxes, wrapping paper, tape, scissors, candy, paper, a pen, newsprint, and a marker.

Additional supplies for optional activities: a large box, small pieces of cardboard, various art supplies, ornament hooks, and a small Christmas tree.

Choose Your Opener

Opener Option 1: Pop Quiz

Have students form pairs. Say: **To begin our meeting today, I'm going to give you a pop quiz. Don't worry—you won't be graded. This quiz will help you think about what Christmas means in your life. After I ask each question, think about your answer, then discuss it with your partner.** Ask:

- How does your life change during the Christmas season? (a) not at all; (b) it gets really busy; (c) I spend more time at church.
- How do you think most people view the meaning of Christmas? (a) time for family; (b) getting and giving gifts; (c) worshipping God for sending Jesus to earth.
- What is most significant to you about Christmas? (a) spending time with family; (b) getting and giving gifts; (c) worshipping God for sending Jesus to earth.

Say: **Today we're going to talk about the meaning of Christmas and how it can change the way we live.**

Opener Option 2: A Tradition

After students arrive say: **I'm going to read some information to you and ask you some questions about Saint Nicholas. Saint Nicholas, who lived in the fourth century, was—according to legend—a native of what is now Turkey. Tradition says he was a monk and an archbishop who secretly gave gifts to three daughters of a poor man who could not afford to pay for his daughters to get married. Because the man didn't have enough money, he was about to give his daughters over to be prostitutes. Saint Nicholas' gifts kept them from this fate. From this tradition grew the custom of filling stockings with secret gifts on Christmas Eve. Santa Claus, of course, is the American version of Saint Nicholas.** Ask:

- **Does the legend of Santa Claus, or Saint Nicholas, reflect the true meaning of Christmas? If so, how?**
- **How has this tradition affected the way you celebrate Christmas?**
- **What's the true meaning of Christmas?**

Say: **Today we're going to talk about the meaning of Christmas and how it can change the way we live.**

Bible Experience: God Has Given...

You'll need Bibles, the small gift-wrapped boxes you prepared before the meeting, tape, and the questions you wrote on newsprint.

Have students form four groups. Be sure each group has at least one Bible.

Give each group one of the gift-wrapped boxes you prepared beforehand.

Tape up the sheet of newsprint with the questions written on it. Instruct each group to open its gift-wrapped box, enjoy the gift you've placed inside, then spend ten minutes reading the Scripture passage, studying what it says, and discussing the questions on the newsprint.

After ten minutes have volunteers share what they learned in their groups. Ask:

- **What is the difference between the gifts in your box and the gifts you read about in Scripture?**
- **How did it feel to receive a short-lasting gift?**
- **How did that feeling compare to the feeling you receive when you understand the eternal gifts God wants to give all of us?**
- **How do you think the gifts God has given us should affect the way we celebrate Christmas?**

Reflection: I Can Give...

Say: **If God has given us such wonderful gifts, Christmas should be a time of responding to those gifts.** Ask:

- **What are some ways we can respond to the gifts God has given us at Christmas?**
- **How can we imitate God's gifts to us?**
- **What are some gifts we can give that people may not see, touch, or feel, but that will last forever?**
- **What are some gifts you can give to others that reflect the gifts God has given to you?**

Choose Your Closing

Closing Option 1: Great Gift Ideas

You'll need a marker and the large gift-wrapped box you prepared before the meeting.

Encourage students to brainstorm ways they, as a group, can give eternal gifts to others, such as raising money for local underprivileged kids or reading to nursing home residents. As they share ideas, write them on the outside of the gift-wrapped box you prepared before the meeting.

Then encourage teenagers to choose one or two of the ideas and commit to carrying them out. If you have time, you may want to help teenagers carry out an idea during or after your meeting time. If not, be sure to make a specific plan for carrying out at least one idea in the future.

LEADER TIP

If you have a large group and feel like your small groups are too big, have students form more than four groups (prepare a few extra boxes in preparation for this). Assign some or all of the Scripture references to more than one group.

Closing Option 2: Gift-mas Tree

You'll need small pieces of cardboard, various art supplies, ornament hooks, and a small Christmas tree.

Give each person a small piece of cardboard, and instruct students to use the cardboard and art supplies to create a Christmas ornament. Students should decorate their ornaments with symbols, pictures, and words that describe gifts they can give to others in response to the gifts God has given them. Say: **Be sure your ornament represents specific ways you personally can respond to God's gifts with gifts of your own.**

When students have finished making their ornaments, have them use ornament hooks to hang their ornaments on a small Christmas tree. Allow students to spend some time looking at the ornaments, and encourage them to ask questions about the ornaments others have created. Then have students form a circle around the tree. Pray aloud, asking God to help teenagers spend the Christmas season giving gifts to others, just as God has given to them.

Leave the tree up in your meeting area for several weeks.

Scripture Index

Theme Index

Group Publishing, Inc.
Attention: Product Development
P.O. Box 481
Loveland, CO 80539
Fax: (970) 679-4370

Evaluation for
HIGH-ENERGY MEETINGS FOR YOUNG TEENAGERS

Please help Group Publishing, Inc., continue to provide innovative and useful resources for ministry. Please take a moment to fill out this evaluation and mail or fax it to us. Thanks!

● ● ●

1. As a whole, this book has been (circle one)

not very helpful   very helpful

1   2   3   4   5   6   7   8   9   10

2. The best things about this book:

3. Ways this book could be improved:

4. Things I will change because of this book:

5. Other books I'd like to see Group publish in the future:

6. Would you be interested in field-testing future Group products and giving us your feedback? If so, please fill in the information below:

Name _____

Street Address _____

City _____ State _____ Zip _____

Phone Number _____ Date _____

Permission to photocopy this page granted for local church use.
Copyright © Group Publishing, Inc., P.O. Box 481, Loveland, CO 80539.

core belief

Bible Study Series

Give Your Teenagers a Solid Faith Foundation That Lasts a Lifetime!

Here are the *essentials* of the Christian life—core values teenagers *must* believe to make good decisions now...and build an *unshakable* lifelong faith. Developed by youth workers like you...field-tested with *real* youth groups in *real* churches...here's the meat your kids *must* have to grow spiritually—presented in a fun, involving way!

Each 4-session **Core Belief Bible Study Series** book lets you easily...
● Lead deep, compelling, *relevant* discussions your kids won't want to miss...
● Involve teenagers in exploring life-changing truths...
● Help kids create healthy relationships with each other—and you!

Plus you'll make an *eternal difference* in the lives of your kids as you give them a solid faith foundation that stands firm on God's Word.

Here are the Core Belief Bible Study Series titles already available...

Senior High Studies

Why **Authority** Matters	0-7644-0892-5	Why **Prayer** Matters	0-7644-0893-3
Why **Being a Christian** Matters	0-7644-0883-6	Why **Relationships** Matter	0-7644-0896-8
Why **Creation** Matters	0-7644-0880-1	Why **Serving Others** Matters	0-7644-0895-X
Why **Forgiveness** Matters	0-7644-0887-9	Why **Spiritual Growth** Matters	0-7644-0884-4
Why **God** Matters	0-7644-0874-7	Why **Suffering** Matters	0-7644-0879-8
Why **God's Justice** Matters	0-7644-0886-0	Why **the Bible** Matters	0-7644-0882-8
Why **Jesus Christ** Matters	0-7644-0875-5	Why **the Church** Matters	0-7644-0890-9
Why **Love** Matters	0-7644-0889-5	Why **the Holy Spirit** Matters	0-7644-0876-3
Why **Our Families** Matter	0-7644-0894-1	Why **the Last Days** Matter	0-7644-0888-7
Why **Personal Character** Matters	0-7644-0885-2	Why **the Spiritual Realm** Matters	0-7644-0881-X
		Why **Worship** Matters	0-7644-0891-7

Junior High/Middle School Studies

The Truth About **Authority**	0-7644-0868-2	The Truth About **Serving Others**	0-7644-0871-2
The Truth About **Being a Christian**	0-7644-0859-3	The Truth About **Sin and Forgiveness**	0-7644-0863-1
The Truth About **Creation**	0-7644-0856-9		
The Truth About **Developing Character**	0-7644-0861-5	The Truth About **Spiritual Growth**	0-7644-0860-7
The Truth About **God**	0-7644-0850-X	The Truth About **Suffering**	0-7644-0855-0
The Truth About **God's Justice**	0-7644-0862-3	The Truth About **the Bible**	0-7644-0858-5
The Truth About **Jesus Christ**	0-7644-0851-8	The Truth About **the Church**	0-7644-0899-2
The Truth About **Love**	0-7644-0865-8	The Truth About **the Holy Spirit**	0-7644-0852-6
The Truth About **Our Families**	0-7644-0870-4	The Truth About **the Last Days**	0-7644-0864-X
The Truth About **Prayer**	0-7644-0869-0	The Truth About **the Spiritual Realm**	0-7644-0857-7
The Truth About **Relationships**	0-7644-0872-0	The Truth About **Worship**	0-7644-0867-4

Order today from your local Christian bookstore, or write:
Group Publishing, P.O. Box 485, Loveland, CO 80539.

Exciting Resources for Your Youth Ministry

All-Star Games From All-Star Youth Leaders

The ultimate game book—from the biggest names in youth ministry! All-time no-fail favorites from Wayne Rice, Les Christie, Rich Mullins, Tiger McLuen, Darrell Pearson, Dave Stone, Bart Campolo, Steve Fitzhugh, and 21 others! You get all the games you'll need for any situation. Plus, you get practical advice about how to design your own games and tricks for turning a *good* game into a *great* game!

ISBN 0-7644-2020-8

Last Impressions: Unforgettable Closings for Youth Meetings

Make the closing moments of your youth programs powerful and memorable with this collection of Group's best-ever low-prep (or no-prep!) youth meeting closings. You get over 170 favorite closings, each tied to a thought-provoking Bible passage. Great for anyone who works with teenagers!

ISBN 1-55945-629-9

The Youth Worker's Encyclopedia of Bible-Teaching Ideas

Here are the most comprehensive idea-books available for youth workers. With more than 365 creative ideas in each of these 400-page encyclopedias, there's at least one idea for every book of the Bible. You'll find ideas for retreats and overnighters...learning games...adventures...special projects...affirmations... parties...prayers...music...devotions...skits...and more!

Old Testament   ISBN 1-55945-184-X
New Testament   ISBN 1-55945-183-1

PointMaker™ Devotions for Youth Ministry

These 45 PointMakers™ help your teenagers discover, understand, and apply biblical principles. Use PointMakers as brief meetings on specific topics or slide them into any youth curriculum to make a lasting impression. Includes handy Scripture and topical indexes that make it quick and easy to select the perfect PointMaker for any lesson you want to teach!

ISBN 0-7644-2003-8

More Resources for Your Youth Ministry

Group's Best Discussion Launchers for Youth Ministry

Here's the definitive collection of Group's best-ever discussion launchers! You'll get hundreds of thought-provoking questions kids can't resist discussing…compelling quotes that demand a response…and quick activities that pull kids into an experience they can't wait to talk about. Add zing to your youth meetings…revive meetings that are drifting off-track…and comfortably approach sensitive topics like AIDS, war, cults, gangs, suicide, dating, parents, self-image, and more!

ISBN 0-7644-2023-2

You-Choose-the-Ending Skits for Youth Ministry

Stephen Parolini

Try these 19 hot-topic skits guaranteed to keep your kids on the edge of their seats—because each skit has 3 possible endings! You can choose the ending…flip a coin…or let your teenagers vote. No matter which ending you pick, you'll get a great discussion going about a topic kids care about! Included: no-fail discussion questions!

ISBN 1-55945-627-2

No Supplies Required Crowdbreakers & Games

Dan McGill

This is the perfect book for youth workers on a tight budget. The only supplies you'll need for these quick activities are kids! All 95 ideas are fun, easy-to-do, creative, and tested for guaranteed success!

ISBN 1-55945-700-7

Youth Worker's Idea Depot™

Practical, proven ideas gathered from front-line professionals make this CD-ROM a gold mine of ministry solutions! You can search these ideas instantly—by Scripture…topic…key words…or by personal notes you've entered into your database. You'll get a complete library of ideas—plus a trial subscription to Group Magazine, where you'll discover dozens of new ideas in every issue! For Windows 3.1 or Windows 95.

ISBN 0-7644-2034-8

Order today from your local Christian bookstore, or write: Group Publishing, P.O. Box 485, Loveland, CO 80539.